UPGRADITIS

UPGRADITIS
An Antidote For Herd Mentality

SANDEEP BABBAR

Copyright © 2022 Sandeep Babbar
All rights reserved.
ISBN- 13: 978-0-646-85540-0

DEDICATION

I am dedicating this to my son, Samar. This book offers all the good advice that a father would like to leave behind for the next generation.

Table of Contents

Dedication	**6**
Introduction: The Elephant Story	**8**
1 Get lucky	24
2 The pursuit of unhappiness	46
3 Everyone is not equal	66
4 Modern slavery	82
5 Finding love	104
6 Technology connects	118
7 Perfectly Flawed	138
8 The addiction myth	158
9 Your superpowers	176
10 The web of beliefs	196
About the author	**216**

INTRODUCTION: THE ELEPHANT STORY

❦

I asked my five-year-old son, who is the King of the Jungle?

He answered it's the Elephant dad.

Why?

It's huge, has the strongest muscles, weighs a lot, and can crush almost any animal in the Jungle. Like my son, all animal lovers would refer to them as the King of the Jungle.

Of course, we all know that is incorrect because Elephants are vegans; they don't hunt or kill; instead, they are salad lovers. Salad lovers are not threatening enough to be the King of the Jungle.

An African elephant can lift objects weighing up to 400 kilograms with its trunk. They are mighty creatures, with more than a hundred thousand muscles and tendons distributed down the length of their trunk; at this level of strength, they can uproot fully mature trees. In addition, they can carry the equivalent of 130 adult humans on their backs. They are mother nature's bulldozers; no one dares to meddle with them; they are truly majestic and, for the most part, peaceful.

There is a strong resemblance between elephants and humans regarding cognition and social structure. Elephants are considered among the most intelligent creatures globally by modern ethologists. The brain mass of an elephant is greater than that of any other land mammal. On the other hand, elephants' brains contain an estimated 250 billion neurons. The Elephant's cortex has around one-third the number of neurons as the human brain.

Elephants exhibit a wide range of behaviours related to various cognitive functions, including sorrow, learning, mimicry, play, altruism, and the use of tools. The ability to extend a finger or equivalent as a nonverbal means of communicating an object may also be understood by elephants, as evidenced by previous studies. Primates are also regarded to be equal in this way.

UPGRADITIS

Elephants are regarded as extremely intelligent, and some researchers argue that the human culling of elephants is wrong because of this. According to Aristotle, this animal is "the animal that transcends all others in knowledge and mind".

The reality is that they are not the King of the Jungle. However, if the Jungle had a title called "The peoples champion", then yes, everyone would agree.

I lived in India for the first two decades of my life. I witnessed a man with a stick domesticated these beasts; I saw these natural bulldozers used by humans to transport waste, pull a buggy, provide experience rides outside Mughal gardens, and perform many other labor-intensive activities. In a circus, I witnessed these enormous hunks of muscle dancing to the beat of the ringmaster's staff.

During the summer of 1990, my family travelled to a small town in Punjab to attend a wedding. The streets in this small town were composed of paving bricks, and water drains were exposed on the sides of the road. I was staying at a semi-rural property owned by a relative of mine. When it came to bustle, this small, packed street in front of my relative's house was comparable to Las Vegas Boulevard in caliber.

Upgraditis

It was a busy and engaging street; within 50 meters, you could experience every possible sound, taste, smell, and activity on that street. Some kids were playing cricket on one side of the street, and on the other side, soccer and badminton were on. You could spot elders sitting outside in groups and reading newspapers. Fruit and vegetable hawkers weaving through and trying to sell their product, not to mention the two-wheeler traffic finding its way through this human circus.

Even though not everyone had televisions in their homes back then, if you were bored, you could come out and sit at your door and watch live street sports, chit chat with neighbours, see kids fight, watch people walk, and experience crazy, unpredictable shit unveiling. There was never a point in time when you felt bored.

Then something unexpected happened while I was standing there watching donkeys transport bricks to a construction site. An unusual sighting was about to occur in my 10-year-old brain, and it was going to be a remarkable event for me. An event that will remain etched in my memory for the foreseeable future and an event that will remain incomprehensible to me for many years to come.

Upgraditis

Out of nowhere, a fully grown Elephant appears on the street, being walked by a man dressed in saffron. Saffron is the colour that denotes faith and courage, which is why it is included on the Indian national flag.

Street elephants are compelled to live and work in urban areas by their owners, who do not care for them. The Elephant's owner or handler makes money by forcing the elephants to perform feats for the general public's enjoyment. They also sell overpriced bananas or other fruit to passersby to supplement their income by feeding the animals.

This man was just carrying a stick, a big saffron bag, and a massive picture of one Hindu God. Elephants also represent a Hindu god, i.e., Ganesha; that is why elephants are considered auspicious in Hindu culture. The Elephant will follow this man everywhere; if the man stops, the Elephant stops. If this elephant man starts walking, the Elephant follows. All the kids on the street were excited to see the Elephant. The kids were making a lot of noise. If the Elephant got distracted, his master would give him a whack on the legs with his stick. The moment it was struck with a stick, the Elephant had an identity crisis. It will start acting like a dog and follow the master obediently without the leash. The kids quickly named the Elephant Raawat, a famous elephant from a Bollywood movie in the '80s.

This man of faith would stop in front of a house and knock on the door; someone would open the door and be amused that the Elephant has shown up on their front door. The family would acknowledge that the man is carrying the photo of their favourite God and what God needs the most is "money", as all Gods do. So, the Elephant man will get some spare change. The Elephant man will shower the family with the verbal blessing and move to the next door, leveraging this giant mammal advertising capital and brand trust of the biggest and finest God in the country.

The family just purchased goodwill and comprehensive insurance against lives uncertainties from their favourite invisible man in the sky. This Elephant man was a marketing genius, walking around and collecting money without even asking it, and it was all tax-free.

This Elephant man struck up a conversation with one of the families on the street, and the family welcomed him inside their home. It is common to practice to feed a man of religion who comes up at your doorsteps in India. As a result, this Elephant man began to prepare to enter the residence.

Unfortunately, this Elephant will not enter the house due to technical difficulties. As a result, he requires a safe location to keep his Elephant. He can't afford to jeopardise his livelihood because he has access to tasty meals in the house.

This man removes a jute rope from his pack and uses it to control the Elephant's movement. He threads the rope through a metal ring that is fastened to a chain wrapped around the Elephant's neck. There was no resistance from the Elephant, and he only had to tug the rope to bring him closer to the door so that he didn't get in the way of the incoming two-wheeler traffic on the street. Next, the Elephant man began looking for locations to secure his three-ton battleship. Amazingly, he simply attached the free end of the rope to the front door handle and walked in to take care of business without anyone noticing. This door handle is secured to the wooden door with four or five tiny screws.

Let me rephrase the situation for you again; we have a 3-ton Elephant on the street, tied with a thin jute rope to a six-inch door handle of an old timber door. I am confident that a fully grown man can kick the door down with not more than five kicks.

Kids are now pelting this Elephant with objects to elicit movement from it. This jungle hero stood there taking abuse from kids who couldn't have weighed more than 25 kilograms each. I kept expecting something to go wrong; I kept expecting the Elephant to tear the door from the hinges, kick these dumb children into outer space, and flee for his freedom. Nothing happened, although it could have at any time.

A few minutes later, the Elephant's master arrives and unties him, pulling the rope from around his neck and strolling away with this magnificent creature trailing close after him. I couldn't fathom how the most powerful animal on the planet could behave in such a meek manner, and I was shocked. But, of course, I was only 10 years old at the time, so that was out of the question. Whatever it was, it had nothing to do with the Elephant's vegan way of life in the slightest. In my case, though, I lacked the life experience essential to appreciate the psychology of this undiscovered potential.

Around 3000 years ago, people began capturing elephants and training them to perform labor-intensive tasks. Initially employed in warfare, they were later used extensively in logging forests, timber yards, land clearing, and the construction of temples. As a result of their utilisation in temples and yards, they have also been used for educational and recreational purposes (e.g., circuses). Although their training comprises traditional ways of establishing dominance, in which punishment plays a key role, much criticism has been levelled against them.

The Gajashastra is a piece of Indian literature that dates to the 5th century and describes various strategies for capturing and training elephants.

In accordance with geographical area and cultural norms, training methods range from severely harsh negative reinforcement to more humane positive support or rewards-based training approaches.

To train an elephant, the most frequent strategy is to first establish control over it through various methods. Forced submission, which is the most common, has attracted widespread condemnation worldwide. The "training crush" method involves tying the Elephant to a wooden post that is firmly planted in the ground with a metal chain. Initial attempts to self-liberate fail, and after a few days, the Elephant's spirit begins to crumble as the bruises around its neck bleed. Finally, the Elephant's spirit is crushed as the Elephant tries and fails to free itself.

> *This animal has now correlated pain with freedom, and as a result, the Elephant will no longer ask for it. When the Elephant refrains from attempting to break free, the Elephant is rewarded.*

Slowly but steadily, this grand 7-ton brute force machine comes to the realisation that if there is a chain around its neck, it will be unable to be free. After a few weeks, the chain connecting to the ground anchor is removed and replaced with a jute rope. The Elephants do not attempt to proceed with the same courage as previously. After a few months, the rope is removed and replaced with a metal strap worn around the neck. There is now an invisible chain preventing the Elephant from moving. The Elephant's sprint has been crushed - The Elephant understands that if this piece of metal is around my neck, I will be unable to escape.

Now, this people's champion of the Jungle walks behind a morally bankrupt man of faith holding a picture of God and collecting loose change from insecure people who fear the invisible man in the sky. Trust in the relationship with fear can been found at all levels.

Two decades after observing Raawat on the street, who was being walked around like a dog, I also noticed similar behaviour in human beings. Humans are born with an unbounded amount of potential. At the very least, we are the champions of this solar system. We can exist and progress in an infinite number of ways; therefore, we refer to a human as "human beings."

I saw humans with unlimited potential chained to their belief systems managed by their version of Elephant man. Society punished them somehow when they tried to break free; slowly, the human sprint was being crushed in these men and women. Those invisible chains of belief systems became bigger and bigger as society progressed. As a result, the human desire for exploration, adventure, expression, and freedom became smaller as I grew old.

I see grown-up humans with boundless potential and talent struggling to make it in this world. Nonetheless, these men and women were subjected to a "training crush" program supported by educational institutions, places of employment, bosses, governments, belief systems, religion, and social rules to crush their desire for exploration and adventure.

In this way, society demonstrates its nature; the myths that society has imposed on you can tie you into invisible chains. We've all had incidents in our lives that have thrown a wrench in our notions of who and what we are. But unfortunately, someone else can write your story if they say that you can't do something and you believe them.

Instead of "let's do it," I hear statements like "I can't do this because" and other self-limiting ideas more often. This is the result of the training crush program that you participated in.

> *The world will ask you who you are; if you don't know, then the world will tell you.*

We must learn more about ourselves and develop more self-awareness and self-observation skills to identify and break free from these invisible bonds and live our best lives.

We are all walking around with limiting notions about ourselves, just like Raawat; we are utterly unconscious of our own abilities and potential and unaware of our own cognitive power. Following the elephant man is something we have learned to do with the help of some invisible chains. Such chains may be known by other names, such as mediocre pay, job insecurity, an abusive but secure relationship (or a combination of the two), phobias and worries, addictions, substance dependence, and even pleasure-seeking habits. You have been chained to a door handle by hundreds of self-limiting beliefs that have been imposed on you by society throughout your life. Society put those chains around your neck by deceiving you.

Instead, think of yourself as the Elephant and envision yourself as such. In this case, it is not a domesticated elephant from down the street, but a wild African savannah beast known as "The People's Champion" of the Jungle. The Elephant with God-like strength may accomplish anything if not hindered by any self-limiting chains, whether real or virtual.

Make a note of the shackles that society has placed around your neck and begin to remove them one at a time as you see fit. The greater the number of chains you destroy, the faster you will reach the escape velocity from the planet mediocrity.

Upgraditis

The chain of fear that society has wrapped around your neck has tethered you to your limiting beliefs and kept you under control.

You are afraid of being wounded if you break free; the unknown is scary, so people get comfortable with their pain, as the pain is known and familiar.

Invisible chains are challenging to deal with because we can't see them, they can continue to reverberate in our brains long after the person or organisation who placed them on us has ceased to play a significant role in our lives.

Invisible bonds can be undone, but first, you must admit that they exist, understand where they originated from, and recognise that they do not reflect your inner self correctly.

When you are not living your most true life, invisible chains can bind you and force you to conform. Invisible chains can entangle and bind people. They have the potential to influence your self-perception, the connections you form, the decisions you make, and the risks you take on in your life. What type of reality do you create for yourself is based on vulnerabilities that have been thrust upon you by someone else's? Such reality is a restricted reality.

There are a variety of approaches to breaking invisible chains, and most of the time, they involve taking action. For example, a new job for some means quitting a relationship; for others, it means admitting a mistake; and for others still, it means starting a new career. The resources are available to you to break your invisible chains and take a good step ahead, but you must actively seek them out.

This book outlines ten self-limiting myths that society forces you to believe, and it will assist you in identifying the Elephant man in your life and resolving the conflict between you and them.

Don't make the same mistake as Raawat.

With this book, I hope to instil a sense of intellectual contagion among the readers, questioning the lies that society has indoctrinated them with. The book is jam-packed with contagious positive concepts and cutting-edge modern wisdom that will inspire you to develop an unquenchable drive to upgrade your life and discover new positivity and emotional development patterns.

1
GET LUCKY

Upgraditis

Two gentlemen came face to face for the first time one fantastic day. Unfortunately, one of the men appeared to be truly depressed. As a result, the other man inquired, "What happened?"

With tears in his eyes, the first man stated, "My first wife passed away from COVID last year. Then, by some miracle, I found love again, but after my second marriage was solemnised, I discovered that my wife had an adulterous affair with my best friend, which devastated me. Earlier this year, my son went to prison because he attempted to murder his step mum. My sixteen-year-old daughter is now expecting a child, and we have no way of knowing the father. To make matters worse, I was forced to evacuate my home when a tropical hurricane slammed the area a few weeks ago. A few days ago, I lost 80% of my investment portfolio because the company I was involved in had gone bankrupt. Today my doctor called and advised that I have cancer".

The other man said, "Wow! that is a long list of unfortunate events that have happened with you in such a short time. Anyway, what do you do for work?

The man replied, "I sell lucky gemstones."

In today's culture, the concept of luck is one of the most pervasive misconceptions that is imposed on everyone by society. In our society, "luck" is the phrase used to explain away our achievements and failures on a timescale. Societal conditioning makes us believe in luck, which is a ridiculous concept. As a result, society stunts our development and prohibits us from reaching our full human potential.

Some evidence suggests that believing in luck has the same effect as taking a placebo, causing people to think favourably or unfavourably and respond more positively or negatively to events.

Some people purposefully put themselves in settings that boost their chances of having a fortuitous meeting, such as socialising with people who work in other fields or networking with people who work in different areas. So, the harder some individuals strive to achieve success, the more fortunate they become. For example, Elon Musk was fortunate because he spent two decades developing ideas to revolutionise the world. Many people may not have the capacity to work 100-hour weeks, but Bill Gates had the passion of doing so because of his vision.

Upgraditis

Luck favours those who don't put their faith in it.

Speaking with failure, success is merely the result of luck.

What society refers to as "luck" can be divided into four categories:

1. ACT OF GOD:

These occurrences seem to come out of nowhere and with no prior notice to the people. This is the kind of luck with which you are usually accustomed. Take into consideration the probability of a miracle, an "Act of God," or winning the big lottery jackpot.

Even though they are something to be thankful for, they are not something in which to place your trust. On the other hand, consider the possibility of a freak accident involving one of your loved ones or of lightning striking your home and destroying it entirely. Many people feel that you cannot produce anything like this out of thin air because of the nature of this form of luck; it comes to you when you least expect it. Was it your luck or just a random chance of possibility?

2. Explorers' success:

This type of luck favours those who have a solid and persistent curiosity about various topics, coupled with a strong desire to experiment and explore.

This type of good fortune comes because of continual exploration. The more stuff you explore, the more people you meet and the more relationships you build, the greater the likelihood that the right person will take notice of you. Perseverance, hard work, motion, action, innovation, and exploration are all necessary ingredients for this kind of good fortune. This kind of fortune is perhaps the most readily available to you currently. This results from the ability to act, which results in good luck.

> *Please keep in mind that doing nothing is a guaranteed way to get unlucky. A little imperfect activity is preferable to a lot of perfect inaction.*

3. EXPLICIT KNOWLEDGE:

Individuals with solid knowledge and particular ability in seeing, memorising, relaying, and swiftly applying specific knowledge will favour this kind of luck. As a result of years of experience, you will be far more knowledgeable about your profession than someone relatively new to it. You will know what works and what doesn't. With time and practice, you become incredibly adept at identifying good fortune.

Consider the following scenario: you are a filmmaker who comes across a book that would make a fantastic film. You already know it would make a terrific movie because you've done similar projects in the past. Anyone who only reads the book will lack the necessary experience and understanding to transform it into a fantastic film.

If you were familiar with cryptography in the early 2010s, it's possible that you would have seen the potential in Bitcoin because you were aware of the ramifications of holding such an asset; you could have stocked up on it for a few pennies. Indeed, you'd be a billionaire right now.

Build specific expertise and experience in your profession to unlock this kind of good fortune. Then keep an eye out for happenings out of the ordinary in your field of expertise. Keep abreast of industry developments, and if you come across an opportunity that appears to be viable, pursue it with tenacity. When an opportunity falls in love with your level of knowledge, this type of luck is born.

4. Unique skill:

It is this type of luck that benefits those who have distinctive, if not outlandish, interests, lifestyles, and habits. The final kind of luck is the strangest and most challenging to come by. As you get closer and closer to expert status, how you behave yourself will become more and more well-known. Perhaps you have a warm and easy-going demeanour that others enjoy working with. Alternatively, you can be extraordinarily focused and always manage to complete your tasks on time, no matter what time it is. These "distinctive" characteristics will aid in the development of your reputation and brand over time. As time goes on, your reputation is like a magnet that only becomes stronger. As you create a loyal customer base, you'll be able to attract more and more business from further and farther away. As time progresses, you'll get closer and closer to becoming regarded as the "best" in the world at what you do.

Eventually, a career-changing customer - someone who admires your personality and worldview - will recruit you for a task that only you are qualified to execute. There you have it: a little bit of good fortune.

This is where you develop a distinctive personality, a distinctive brand, and distinctive thinking, and it is here that luck finds you. You must create a talent stack that is exclusive to you. The greater the number of skills you accumulate, the more distinctive your offering becomes, and the greater the likelihood that you will become the "best" at something.

Continue to explore what you are interested in and develop your skills in those areas. You'll make it to the top of the world because you're the only person on the planet who can do what you can do. Because you have chosen not to be a rival, you have selected to be in a market for one.

Finding money on the street may appear to be a lucky break, but it is more accurate to suggest that you should thank yourself for your good fortune rather than anyone else. Numerous studies have attempted to determine whether luck can be objectively measured and have had various degrees of success in their efforts. A number of these studies have discovered that the perception of "luck" has more to do with psychology than it does with possibilities; Actually, "good luck" is nothing more than your own optimistic thinking, which keeps you open to new prospects and recognises patterns in seemingly random acts of opportunity.

A well-known psychologist conducted a decade-long empirical investigation into why certain people appear to lead charmed lives full of fortunate encounters. On the other hand, others seem to be experiencing multiple tragedies. The psychologist was particularly interested in learning more about the "science of luck". Moreover, the professor wanted to recruit both lucky and unlucky people for this study to get it off the ground. So, he published an advisement for recruiting both lucky and unlucky people for the study.

He recruited 200 unlucky people who believed life was unfair and that everything they touched turned to garbage. They were dealing with shattered relationships, career difficulties, and economic hardship, and they had lost all the games that life had attempted to play with them. For all intents and purposes, he was hunting for 200 losers who had been caught in the clutches of life.

Upgraditis

He also recruited 200 very fortunate people. People who are successful in their professions get promoted swiftly. People who had achieved significant financial success had excellent interpersonal relationships and were successful in all aspects of their lives. These were the individuals who had seized all opportunities that life had presented to them.

His ambition was to have a better understanding of the science of luck. As a result, over several years, he observed these 400 exceptional men and women, ranging in age from 18 to 84, who were selected from all areas of life for this one experiment.

Both the lucky and unlucky groups were given a newspaper during one of the studies. Both the groups were instructed to count the number of photographs published inside the newspaper, and the individual and group times will be recorded. On average, it took the unlucky group approximately two minutes to count the number of photographs. On the other hand, the lucky group only needed a few seconds to count the number of photos in the newspaper.

This was made possible by a message in bold script on page three of the newspaper, which stated, "Stop counting; there are 43 photographs in this newspaper." This was why lucky people were able to dominate in this study.

The lucky group was simply doing something above and beyond what they were instructed to.

They were just not looking for photographs; they also casually eyeballed the text on the page.

Just for kicks, the psychologist also included a second significant statement in the newspaper, which was placed halfway through the publication. It told them to stop counting. Inform the experimenter that you have observed this, and you will receive two hundred and fifty dollars. The unlucky individuals missed out on this occasion because they were still preoccupied with their search for images.

Researchers discovered that luck is neither a mystical ability nor the outcome of random chance, as previously believed. People are not born with good fortune. Instead, it is the beliefs and actions of individuals that account for much of their good or bad luck.

Researchers discovered that luck has more to do with our own thinking than with any external causes and that lucky people produce their own good fortune by following four simple guidelines.

- Make the most of new opportunities: Fortunate people are adept at spotting and capitalising on new opportunities. Lucky people accomplish this through networking, maintaining a laid-back attitude about life, and being open to new experiences.

- Paying attention to their instincts: Lucky people often make decisions based on intuition and gut feelings. Meditating and clearing their minds through reading or writing can further enhance their intuitive powers.

- Be prepared for awesome things to happen: Fortunate people believe that the future will be filled with lovely things. These expectations, on the other hand, become self-fulfilling prophecies. These expectations also assist them in confidently dealing with failure.

- Ability to turn bad luck into a good perspective: They realise how things could have been much worse, but they do not dwell on their misfortune and instead choose to take control of the situation they find themselves in. Athletes who earn bronze medals consider themselves lucky than those who win silver medals in competition. The silver medalists are fixated on the concept that they might have taken home a gold medal if they performed just a little better. On the other hand, the bronze medalists are preoccupied with the notion that if they had performed even slightly worse, they would not have won anything at all. It is called "counterfactual" thinking when we think about what might have happened instead of what happened. This explains how lucky people who have been fortunate use counterfactual reasoning to lessen the emotional impact of the bad things they've had to deal with in their own lives.

It is true that some people are just born with advantages and that events occur in our life that is entirely out of our control, but this is not the case for everyone. Opening oneself up to new experiences, practicing gratitude, and taking a step outside of your comfort zone increase your chances of success.

UPGRADITIS

The psychologist who conducted the investigation discovered that lucky individuals have much more wonderful extroversion scores than the general population. They also smile twice as often as the unlucky group and make twice as much eye contact. Because of their sociability, individuals are more likely to encounter a fortunate opportunity because they meet more people, interact with them more effectively, and establish meaningful relationships.

Unlucky people are simple to identify because they will be anxious and moan about how everything is rigged, how the system is flawed, and how society has marginalised them. They won't shut up or listen to other people's points of view, and they lack a vision or a solution to the problem. They're the ones I refer to as the Hippos. Just go get your phone and look up Hippo face on Google right now. You may observe that the Hippo has short ears, tiny eyes, and a vast mouth, all of which indicate the attributes of someone unlucky in life. Small eyes indicate a lack of vision, a large mouth suggests someone skilled at verbal diarrhoea, and small ears indicate someone who will not listen to others. Avoid such Hippos at all costs; their tendencies will inevitably rub off on you, and you may find yourself in an unfortunate situation.

While the lucky people were winning in the game, the unlucky got together and started a new stream of a belief system called the "power of superstition". This has been going on for centuries. The unfortunate people have been working very hard; they have invented charms, amulets, talismans, praying and many superstitions.

Superstition comes from when people thought that luck was a strange force that could only be controlled by magical rituals, divine intervention, and bizarre traditions. If a cat crosses your path, it should not imply bad luck - instead, it signifies that the cat is going somewhere. For some people, it is bad luck to fall out of a 13-storey building on a Friday.

Superstition is to knowledge what astrology is to astronomy, the crazy daughter to a wise mother.

People who believe in luck believe in fate as well. They must understand that humans are not objects; they are beings. Things, not people, have a fate. A stool can have a fate; it will fulfil that purpose as it was made for a specific purpose. Consciousness exists in humans. Consciousness can't have a fate. Consciousness can select what it wants to be. Fate has the connotation of being the exact opposite of freedom. You were born a slave; according to fate, your servitude stamp was sealed entirely even before you were born; perhaps you were brainwashed by society. Fate is another bullshit product developed by society.

Astrologers, tarot cards, and psychic readers exploit mankind because of this belief in fate. If you didn't believe in fate, they wouldn't have been able to take advantage of you. If you have a fate, they might be able to find it in the lines on your hands, the lines on your head, inside some cards, or in your birth chart, which contains the combination and position of stars and planets. I'm sure there's a method to read the code. The strangest part is that you seem to enjoy these frauds predicting your fate. You're way too curious to learn about the future, even if knowing about the future entails that you'll die.

How can there be freedom if the future is already decided? If something is going to happen tomorrow, it will happen tomorrow. If we are just victims of some unknown force, we are not in charge of ourselves. You are not your own master if you believe you have a fate. Your life is entirely out of your hands. Fate has all kinds of implications, and this is just one of them. You become a slave because of it. Therefore, if everything is predetermined, there isn't much thrill; you are no longer necessary in your own life. So, it's not even accurate to refer to it as your own life.

To be fully conscious, you must assume full responsibility for your life and put yourself in charge of every aspect of it. Your life needs a mindful and curious re-creation. The stars and planets from astrology and numerology aren't your friends, and neither is Fengshui, Tarot cards and psychic readers. Avoid letting such nonsense get into your head since once you get into this rut, you'll be unable to do anything in life. It will limit your potential as a human being.

There is a missing variable in the luck equation called time. Time gives us perspective on luck. For example, good luck today may result in bad luck in the long term and vice versa.

A small story below gives you a perspective on the importance of time.

Once upon a time, a farmer and his son had a beloved stallion who helped the family earn a living. Then, one fine day, the horse ran away, and their neighbours said, "Your horse ran away; that's bad luck!". So, the farmer replied, "Let us see." A few days later, the horse returned from the wild; this time around, this horse was followed by a few wild mares. The neighbours shouted out, "Now you have so many horses. That's good luck!" and the farmer replied, "let us see. "Later that week, the farmer's son tried to train one of the mares, and she kicked him hard, breaking his bone in the leg. The neighbour cried, "Your son's leg is broken; that's bad luck!". The farmer replied, "Let us see." After a week, soldiers from the army marched through town, recruiting all the physically fit young men to serve in the military since the war had officially begun. Fortunately, the farmer's son wasn't recruited because he was still recovering from the broken bone. His neighbours shouted, "Your boy is safe, that good luck!" to which the farmer replied, "Let us see."

To summarise, life events cannot be classified as good or terrible, fortunate, or unfortunate, at the moment they occur; in many circumstances, only time will reveal all the facts of the situation.

In the same way, that the neighbour was tempted to invest significant time and effort into establishing beliefs that appear fantastic on the surface, but which may not hold up over time. Additionally, we can be tempted to pass judgement on aggravating circumstances or transient displeasure as if it were the end of the world if we think about it too much.

People who practice mindfulness remain curious about their experiences by noticing how they feel emotionally and observing what thoughts are going through their heads. Practicing curiosity in life can help you avoid the 'autopilot' habit of judging experiences as either good or bad luck. Curiosity also enables you to approach uncertainty in your everyday life positively. Don't become a submissive victim to the circumstances that life puts your way.

Considering the farmer's approach reminds me of one of the famous book authors who coined the term Circles of Influence & Circle of Concern. This mental model aimed to encourage people to become conscious of spending their life's energy. You can waste your energy by worrying about problems you can't change, or you can apply it to be more proactive about your life. The circle of concern encompasses all your daily worries about the world, weather, and politics. The circle of influence is a circle within the circle of concern, and it includes the issues you actually have some influence over, like your health, family, and skill.

Upgraditis

We need to upgrade ourselves to clearly see the distinction between these two circles within their own lives; focusing more on what sits within their circle of influence helps them take practical action that enhances life. Combining this with mindfulness means that rather than always passing judgment on things and declaring them as good or bad, you can shift some thinking habits and see this world correctly, which can be incredibly empowering.

When you live your life by chance, you will instil feelings of worry and anxiety in yourself. However, when you conduct your life based on curiosity, aim, skill and capability, you are at least in command of what is happening within you. Life becomes steadier because of this choice. So, pay attention and stop whining about your bad luck because it's time to upgrade your way of thinking.

> *The less we are deserving of good fortune,*
> *the more you will expect it. This is because*
> *good luck favours those who are mentally*
> *prepared.*

So, if you want good fortune, fail more, expect good things, do better, hire smart people, invest, work hard, build meaningful relationships, stop complaining, be proactive, be honest to yourself and others, scatter kindness, smile more, act, accept responsibility, master your skills, trust your gut, take the leap, develop patience, stay curious and don't try; instead, un-try.

> *If you look at a flowering bush and a thorny bush in nature, you will notice that all honeybees are drawn to the bush with flowers. This does not imply that the shrub with flowers is lucky; it simply indicates that it contains nectar, which you may not be able to detect from a distance. People avoid the bush because it has thorns; it is uncomfortable to be around it. Both shrubs are utterly unaware of what they are producing. If you are naturally drawn to certain things, they will gravitate towards you.*

THE PURSUIT OF UNHAPPINESS

Upgraditis

Happiness is a trap, and society begins preparing you for it early. This myth of perfect happiness stems from the stories told to us in childhood. We relate to these stories because, for many of us, they symbolise the dream we strive for in our own lives: a world free of misery, pain, and fear. But, unfortunately, the problem with this idealised state is that the more we pursue it, the more miserable and dissatisfied we become.

The generalised form of plastic happiness that we experience every day is an American invention. Russians believed, "a person who smiles a lot is either an American or a fool." Before the 18th century, almost all cultures encouraged their populations to maintain a melancholic demeanour, and public smiling or another emphatic expression of joy was not usual. This doesn't mean that people were actually unhappy. On the contrary, expression of happiness and the pursuit of happiness was non-existent in society.

At the very least, a dramatic transition happened in Western society some 250 years ago. The beginning of the rise of happiness may be traced back to the United States Declaration of Independence, which stated that all men have a right to "the pursuit of happiness." In a few decades, the smiling American man had become a universal caricature throughout the world. This changed a lot in the 1800s, when Alexander Pope said, "Oh happiness! our being's end and aim!". Once the idea gained momentum, people started writing about their desire to be happy. It was now okay to look for happiness.

From the 1920s onwards, there was yet another boom; tremendous literature arose that emphasised the significance of happiness, human responsibility for achieving happiness, and the solutions accessible to mankind.

New norms of conduct for white-collar workers and salesmen emphasised the importance of a happy demeanour. It gave birth to new commercial enterprises like the Walt Disney Company, whose corporate motto became "make people happy," and whose staff persuaded consumers that they were already happy solely because they were in a Disney environment. It also led to new standards for public posing, with smiles all around, whether at family outings or in politicians' mug shots. There was a progressive growth in dentists during this time when individuals were more inclined to smile. It could be possible that the hesitant smile of a Mona Lisa reflected discomfort about dental damage.

The song "Happy Birthday" was composed in 1926, perhaps due to the gloomy atmosphere of the Great Depression and by the late 1930s, it had become a household tradition. After the great depression, consumerism was a significant theme. Advertisers of all kinds recognised the power of connecting products with happiness. This is the most compelling reason why the mid-twentieth-century happiness culture has endured, especially today. Now even the Russians, Germans and Japanese have also started smiling. The Smiley face was invented in 1963, and by the end of the decade, annual licensing costs had surpassed $50 million. In 1977, McDonald's launched the Happy Meal, which is still used today. The happiness we are experiencing is a contemporary product rather than an inherent element of the human mind.

If happiness is an inborn attribute, so telling someone to be happy is like telling them to grow taller.

There is a huge industry built on this thirst for happiness. Countless self-help coaches and publications claim to hold the key to eternal happiness. The pursuit of happiness appears to be one of the most significant aspects of our life today. Some countries are calculating their gross national happiness index now. There are several programmes all over the internet aiming to restore happiness in just five days. However, a five-day happiness program is far-fetched. As soon as you receive your happiness certificate, someone will do or say something that will evoke a different emotion within you, and your happiness will vanish.

The happiness these days can also be downloaded from the internet through a 10-step method, and there are countless apps on the app store devoted just to enhancing happiness. All of this is telling us that we need to be happy. But unfortunately, they're also attempting to convince you that happiness is a destination, which it isn't.

Happiness is an emotion that plays a minor role in our lives. Sadness, optimism, negativity, pride, jealousy, rage, serenity, and thankfulness are also present. All these feelings are a part of who we are. However, none of them is a destination or a location to which we must journey. We shouldn't try to find happiness because doing so will make us feel worse. "I want to be happy", and we constantly repeat over and over in our heads, and when we aren't consistently pleased, we go into a dark place.

Upgraditis

I witnessed Will Smith deliver an Oscar-worthy performance in "The Pursuit of Happyness," a challenging but incredibly rewarding movie. The Pursuit of Happyness, inspired by the true story of Christopher Gardner, is a tearjerker, yet it also manages to inspire and motivate.

"The Pursuit of Happyness," Will Smith plays Chris Gardner, a brilliant salesman struggling to find work despite his skills and abilities. Gardner and his five-year-old kid were evicted from their San Francisco apartment with nowhere else to go because they couldn't make ends meet. For the sake of a better life for himself and his son, Gardner works as an intern at a high-end stock brokerage firm, enduring many hardships, including living in shelters.

When I was watching the movie, I couldn't stop crying. My father sat along and had teary eyes. I witnessed the same outcome with my flatmate. We were all in tears because Will Smith, who has been ostracised his whole life, has finally been offered a job at a brokerage firm after years of struggle. When the movie finishes, he is beaming with fulfilment and tears of happiness, knowing that he will be able to provide for his son's needs for the first time in years. This is the end of the story.

Essentially, Hollywood was feeding you a load of nonsense while also marketing you the world's most overrated product that you should overlook; the product in question is happiness. My recommendation is to avoid chasing it. Get away from people who promise it or try to sell it to you.

Just for fun, let's imagine a sequel called The Pursuit of Happyness 2.

The plot of that film intrigues me. So, let's look at the most probable outcome. As far as I can tell, this is how the story will go.

Will Smith is on his way to work; it's 5 a.m., and his box-shaped clock buzzes; he gets out of his box-shaped bed, gets ready in a box-shaped room, and then opens his box-shaped cereal for an out of box breakfast experience. Jumps in his boxed commute, carrying his boxed lunch to his boxed office. Will Smith now spends his days sitting in front of a box shape monitor, staring at Microsoft excel boxes. When he has 10 minutes free from his boxed routine, he goes to Amazon.com and orders some boxes of things to make his boxed home more satisfying. It's now 5 p.m.

Upgraditis

He needs to hurry to pick up his son from box-care and go by the local Chinese restaurant to get a couple of boxes for supper. The boxed dinners are enjoyed by the father and son while they sit and watch the boxed shaped TV. Finally, it's 8 p.m., and it's time to go to bed. This was a regular day in Will Smith's life in the sequel.

Will Smith decides that he needs a new automobile and house because the old boxes no longer make him happy. As a result, he takes out a car loan and a mortgage to upgrade a few boxes in this life. Because of this, he is feeling less and less satisfied, as the rush of dopamine he previously received from opening new boxes is declining each day. In addition, the box habits are creating financial pressure in Will Smith's life. The only way out of this financial mess is to find a higher-paying job, and fortunately for Will Smith, he now has some work experience under his belt. He has landed a fantastic analyst position in a private equity firm with terrible corporate culture.

Will's new boss is a bully with a strategic agenda; he makes Will Smith work long hours and wants him to produce at a pace of 200 per cent of his previous output. So now Will Smith isn't spending nearly enough quality boxed time with his son, who has begun hanging out with some questionable characters and is now opening other kinds of boxes.

It's 11 p.m. now. Will Smith is still in the office, slaving away on a report to meet the utterly arbitrary deadline imposed by his psychotic boss. The information must be ready by 9 a.m. the following day, or Will Smith's boss will grab him by his balls. He is no longer a man who stands up with courage in the face of mistreatment; he is now negatively leveraged.

> *The moral of the story is that if you chase happiness relentlessly, life will finally grab you by the balls.*

Will Smith had been on the quest for many desires; he thinks he will be happy once his desires are met.

> *In fact, a desire is a contract you make with yourself, in which you agree to be unhappy until you obtain what you seek.*

The greater the number of desires you have, the more uncomfortable contracts you will enter. This is how the hunter-gatherers of happiness drown in their miseries. People cling to the illusion that something, someone or someplace out there, will make them happy and fulfilled for the rest of their lives. Unfortunately, the word "happy" has become increasingly weaponised.

Several things influence one's level of happiness, including successes, objectives, rewards, and so on. However, life is not solely about one's accomplishments and desires; something else lends significance to one's existence. Similarly, various external events can detract from one's ability to feel happy. Finally, remember that the most joyful individuals on the planet don't have the best of everything; instead, they make the most of what they have.

So, why do we spend so much money on nonsense and trade our hard-earned money for fleeting happiness?

Perhaps it's because it's easier to satisfy one's material cravings than to deny them.

You can now purchase your way out of unhappiness. As a result, everyone you see gathering boxes is unhappy. They are attempting to escape unhappiness. If getting boxes made us happy, then the people who walked this globe thousands of years ago would have been unhappy, and we'd all be happy. Despite this, all signs in our modern society indicate a decline in happiness.

> *You will be unhappy if you have the notion that something is missing right now. Your desire to be happy will lead to disappointment. So, once you realise that nothing is missing right now, you will find yourself in a beautiful mental condition.*

For millennia, people worldwide have been renouncing their material possessions and aspirations to become monks. Is that something that makes you happy? No, not at all. If that had worked, then everyone on the earth would have become monks by now.

Monks, in my opinion, are the most self-centred group in human society. They make no contributions to the community, do not educate children, create jobs, discover new treatments or technologies to improve the quality of life, and do not pay taxes. Instead, they seek shelter in the mountains, chanting mantras and becoming a burden on society, giving the illusion that they are on the moral high ground and possess all the solutions to the mysteries of the universe.

Upgraditis

A philosopher in India noted that whenever he meets a prostitute, she talks about spirituality and god. On the other hand, every time he meets with a priest, he wishes to talk about sex.

This implies that whatever you deprive yourself of will eventually become your mental prison.

Monks are in mental confinement due to their refusal to indulge in pleasures.

Happiness is a charlatan's illusion; all the bright people I've encountered in my life have expressed a desire not to be happy.

They understand happiness will make them stupid, lethargic, and less engaged with the journey and purpose of their lives. They are concerned that they will not put out the effort necessary to build a meaningful existence if they get happy.

People turn to recreational drugs, psychedelics, and alcohol to find enjoyment in fleeting moments. In a similar vein, Yogis seek happiness through practices such as meditation, holotropic breathing, and hypnotic techniques. In contrast to this, they are addicted to the pleasure gained from their desired state, which is non-linear in effort and never provides you with a feeling of complete fulfilment.

Your parents, teachers, coaches, peers, and Hollywood have all warped this commodity called happiness, so you'd have figured it out if you're as bright as you believe you are. Or you're looking for something that doesn't exist.

So, the advice I have received from the smartest is don't look for happiness; instead, seek peace.

Not peace of mind but peace from the mind. As a peaceful brain will make better decisions in life. The more peaceful you become, the less likely you screw things upon this planet. All brilliant choices are made with a peaceful mind.

Always check your peace-o-meter before you make big decisions in life. In this information age, all our options are leveraged and compounded. So, we must bring ourselves to a peaceful state before making any decisions. Our brain is the most complex system, and the biggest problem for humans is that it doesn't come with an operating manual. We are making stuff as we go along. One thing is for sure that this complex brain works and perform the best when operated under the peaceful mode.

A peaceful mind doesn't seek pleasures, stays calm, and makes brilliant longer-term decisions. Hang out with people in this state; make them your friends. Peaceful people will never get addicted to any substance, a peaceful mind will not have many desires, a peaceful mind will find joy in little things around them. Next time if someone asks you, Are you happy? You should answer. No, don't want to because I am peaceful.

The moment your mind shuts up, you are in peace from mind territory. For example, this happens when you're viewing a beautiful sunrise over the ocean, having a good time with your children, and doing goofy stuff; when you swim or run for a long time, everything in your head goes quiet. That sense of amazement is lovely, and it provides joy to every cell in your body. Your mind becomes your slave when you're in that state. Unfortunately, when the mind becomes our master, we do things that rob us of our peace; we become the most anxious, worried, and furious beings on the planet.

Upgraditis

It's a common misperception that living in peace makes life dull. It's important to remember that peace doesn't mean being uninteresting; instead, it means being at ease. It increases your sense of well-being, joy, and aliveness. It is possible to fully live one's life when inner peace is found.

During the COVID pandemic lockdowns in Australia, I found peace. We were restricted to our homes, and it became difficult to spend money and buy boxes because businesses were closed. Inactivity became an essential aspect of our life suddenly. We observed ants crawl on the ground while sitting in the bush next to our house with my 4-year-old son. We were intrigued by how they transported food back to their home. We sat in the bush and watched spiders in action; how this spider trapped a fly, killed it with venom, and then began removing the pieces; my son didn't move as we sat in the bush and watched mother nature at play. We'd be in the bush for 3-4 hours gazing at bugs, butterflies, and birds, and it would feel like 3-4 minutes. We were, nevertheless, at ease. I've never experienced such peace in my life.

Upgraditis

A peaceful and content person, when doing nothing, will always be happy. This is because there are no cravings in a peaceful person's life. Instead, a happy person will be anxious, jittery, and full of excitement, followed by a crash and feeling of emptiness.

How do we get to that state? That's the big question. It's a simple thing:

- The inactivity of body and mind is the first step towards peace. To be in this state of mind allows you to better comprehend the world around you, and as a result, those things become ingrained in your personality. If you practice inactivity over time, you'll find that you're able to relax more and more each day. Because of this, it's tough to find peace if you're constantly on the go.

- You might also acquire more peace in life by living below your means. Try to keep your possessions to a minimum. Try to reduce the number of things you own, including clothing, toys, and boxes.

- You can't solve world issues if you avoid reading the news or discussing politics. You should avoid all forms of news because they are detrimental to your mental health.

- Avoid spending time with people who complain a lot or are in constant disagreement with others. It's only a matter of time before they start fighting with you since they're causing so much trouble for everyone else. If they are complaining about everyone, it is only a matter of time before they begin to complain about you as well. People who debate ideas and like intellectual discussions should be hung out with; people who discuss people and events should be kept at a social distance.

I spent a considerable amount of time considering what I truly desired out of life. I realised I wasn't looking for happiness in the traditional sense of the word; instead, I was looking for inner peace. I realised how much I missed taking a break and just being present in the moment. I wasn't really feeling anything at all in those moments, but rather a sense of calm. Those sentiments were far more meaningful to me than the momentary enjoyment that I felt like I had to strive so hard to achieve.

Upgraditis

I began to pay attention to the times and places when I felt at peace, as well as what brought me there. As a result, I became more self-aware and actively sought out these possibilities. I realised that spending time outside and around nature made me feel more at ease, so I've made it a priority to spend more time there. It dawned on me that being disconnected from the internet and other people's problems gave me more peace. I chose a way of life that makes me peaceful. Since becoming more self-aware, I've increased the things in my life that offer me peace and joy while reducing the things that rob me of it. If you've been looking for happiness but can't seem to find it or are always disappointed, you might want to try looking for peace.

Happiness and peace are not the same things:

- Happiness is conditional, whereas peace is unconditional.
- Happiness does not last indefinitely, but peace does.
- The degree of happiness can be quantified, but peace cannot.
- Happiness is a feeling of temporary satisfaction, whereas peace is a feeling of permanent satisfaction.

- Happiness involves manifestation; peace is a tranquil sense of strength.

- Happiness is like romance, flamboyant and insistent, whereas peace is like love, humble and accommodating.

- Happiness is like diving into a turbulent river, whereas peace gently lowers oneself into a tranquil lake.

- Happiness is excitement and loudness seeking more pleasure; peace is a serene, pleasing smile.

- Happiness is positioned on an uncomfortable cliff's edge, while peace lies down in relaxation.

- Happiness craves companionship; peace is delighted with solitude.

- Happiness is immature, carefree, and thoughtless; peace is mature, wiser, and more attentive. Peace is a sensation of stillness; all cravings are fulfilled moral or immoral.

- Everybody turns out or towards someone else to seek happiness, but peace can only be attained when you look within. You cannot acquire peace before analysing your inner nature and your incentives.

Upgraditis

Being happy can be compulsive; it triggers the brain to generate compounds that contribute to an overall false sensation of well-being, emotional arousal, and euphoria. So, when you compare peace and happiness, you'll see that peace is a more powerful emotion.

I am sorry that society tells you so many lies; the happiness myth is one. I wanted to bust that to see that you are chasing a ghost. Look for peace instead, and you will enjoy every day on this planet. Always seek objective truth; seeking peace is seeking truth in life. When you seek peace, all negative habits will disappear.

Do fewer things, and you will have more freedom and peace in life and please don't sell this happiness product to the next generation, so they can find peace earlier in their lives.

EVERYONE IS NOT EQUAL

UPGRADITIS

Marketing slogans are usually misleading; let me list a few for you here.

"Environmentally friendly diesel cars." - Volkswagen.

Volkswagen was fined $15 billion in 2016 for defrauding customers and the federal government.

"Gives you wings." - Red Bull.

In 2014, the corporation agreed to pay $13 million to resolve a class-action lawsuit.

"Shoe that burns calories." - New Balance.

In 2012, New Balance agreed to pay a $2.3 million settlement to resolve allegations that the company had made deceptive promises.

"Rice Krispies boosts immunity." - Kellogg's.

Kellogg's agreed to pay a $2.5 million penalty in 2011 for making blatantly false claims.

"Clinically proven to boost genes." - L'Oréal.

In 2014, L'Oréal was fined and barred from making similar statements about boosting genes in the future.

"Eclipse gum kills germs that cause bad breath." - The Wrigley company.

Chewing gum manufacturer paid $7 million to settle a class-action lawsuit alleging that the gum killed germs.

"Shape up with shoes." - Skechers.

Sketchers was fined $50 million for making deceptive promises about their products' ability to tone the bodies of its consumers.

Slogans promoting products, causes, or ideologies are frequently misleading or based on little or no data. Instead, slogans are catchy phrases used to stimulate our interest by evoking solid feelings about a product, company, cause, social or political ideology. Entities like Fairtrade and federal trade commissions were in place to prevent businesses from using slogans to misrepresent their products. Despite this, no entity was ever established to punish those who create and utilise misleading political or social slogans that misrepresent reality.

When I was growing up, the following slogans began to ring in my ears:

"Everyone is equal."

"Equality for all"

"Equality for everyone"

Everyone is equal is a lie that society has concocted to promote equality. Everything within creation is never equal, and as I gaze around in the cosmos, I see that none of the planets or stars is equal. Likewise, when I look around this globe, I see that no two trees are equal, and that no two rivers, mountains, or countries are equal. None of your family members appears or behaves equally; you all have unequal tastes, interests, potential, money, and talent.

> *Even the fingers on your hands are unequal. It is unlikely that humans would have learned the sensitivity and grip necessary to manufacture any tools if all the fingers were equal. Without a doubt, human evolution would have taken a different path, and we would not have been able to create the world we live in today.*

It's simple: just like no two fingerprints are equal in this world, and you want two human beings to be equal? So, considering this, why do we have gold, silver, and bronze medals since everyone is equal?

Society's misreading and misinterpretation of equality slogans increased dramatically. We didn't even try to refute the bullshit that society fed us one spoon at a time.

Upgraditis

Equality is a fundamental concept: it signifies equal protection under the law, which means that all individuals' rights are protected, and none of those rights is infringed upon. For example, equality means equal opportunity for everyone to work, equal pay for equal work, equal voting rights, equality for marriage, equal law, equal freedom, etc. Equality simply means equal opportunity for all.

When given equal opportunities, free people in society will be free to make unequal choices, which will result in unequal outcomes. Some people will do well, and some won't, and they will end up with unequal outcomes because they made unequal choices. This is true freedom.

> *You can either have equality or freedom, but you can't have both because when one prevails, the other dies.*

When you look at reasonably free cultures, such as democracies, you'll see that there's a lot of disparity. For example, income disparity is a significant problem in all free countries because it accumulates human inequality. In other words, if left unmanaged or unregulated, humankind's inherent nature is inequality.

Upgraditis

Likewise, if you study less free cultures, such as those founded on socialism or communism, you will notice that people are far more equal. Most individuals in socialist or communist states have a similar socioeconomic level. While there is more equality in these cultures, individuals have far less freedom.

So let me state unequivocally that equity and equality are not the same things. Only one syllable separates equity and equality. Individualism vs. tribalism, justice vs. injustice is all symbolised by this one syllable. Equity means equality of outcome, i.e., an external force will be required to determine equal outcomes.

In India, numerous quota systems were born out of a desire for social equity. From primary education to job placement, the society established quotas for people who had previously been disadvantaged due to a lack of opportunity or resources. Quota systems stripped 50% of the opportunities from individuals of distinction and gave them to a group demanding social equity. Although equality of opportunity had always existed in India, it was now more important to ensure equality of outcome. Even though the system is still in place in India, where 50 per cent of seats are reserved for specific communities, brilliant general category people are marginalised.

As a result, India experienced a significant brain drain problem, with hundreds of thousands of talented professionals starting to leave the country to pursue opportunities in other free countries. These general category professionals who left India owing to a lack of equal opportunities rose up the ranks to become the CEOs of companies such as Microsoft, Google, Twitter, Chanel, Adobe, IBM, MasterCard, PepsiCo, Cognizant, Nokia, NetApp, Novartis and most importantly Only fans.

What India did to its population 50 years ago, western culture is now doing to the current generation. As a result, brain drain and a lack of innovation will occur since local systems will be controlled by inept individuals, and talent will be suffocated in the name of equity. This is a deception in which society creates equality slogans and sells you equity. But, unfortunately, the product marketed, promoted, and sold differed from the product received.

Equity discourages hard work and encourages lazy behaviour. A society dominated by lazy people is doubtful to be productive. It makes no sense to work harder if we're all heading to the same destination anyway.

Upgraditis

Equity stifles creativity and innovation.

Equity aided authoritarianism this state is intrinsically unnatural to humans; forcible interventions are necessary to bring everyone to the same level.

Equity produces poor results. If we artificially place less-than-ideal candidates in positions to meet quotas, we'll end up with less-than-ideal decision-making that will impair not only the company's success but also the benefit it provides to everyone.

Consider the scenario: we draw an imaginary line through every group, room, family, team, and place of business in society. In that event, uneven sides will result, with unequal levels of education, income, intellect, sense of humour, mental and physical strength, among other things. To achieve equality, the equity social engineers will promote policy that actively discriminates to resolve unproven discrimination on both sides of the imaginary line.

We need to understand the psychology behind this thought process. Everybody feels inferior to somebody, either physically, intellectually, or financially. We are continually comparing ourselves to others and building inferiority complexes. Somebody has more money, better looks, better body, better health, somebody can run faster than you or think faster, swim faster, make money more quickly. Naturally, if you constantly compare yourself with others, you will feel inferior.

Despite being the greatest conqueror in history, Napoleon was quickly irritated by any reference of his height. He was constantly embarrassed that everyone he encountered was taller than him, and he could not change it.

Once, when he went to hang his armour on the wall, he found that the hook was too high for him to reach. His military commander observed him in distress and stepped in to lend a helping hand.

'His excellency, let me do it for you, as I am higher than you.'

Napoleon said, "You are only taller than me, not higher."

A soldier pierced a deep wound in Napoleon's soul in the blink of an eye. Even individuals with immense power and authority feel inferior when they start comparing. As a result, they develop an inferiority complex and lose their peace of mind. This is precisely why some individuals find communism so appealing.

Upgraditis

Every human being has a fundamental yearning to be treated equally, and communism satisfies that urge.

There will be no wounds; no one will be hurt since there will be no one to compare. The ideology of communism serves as a consolation for those who believe they are inferior somehow. Communist employers, colleges, schools, bosses, sports teams, and even movie studios are easy to spot because their enthusiasm for forced equality and promoting equality of outcome stifles meritocratic values.

As I grew older, I witnessed the social equality movement was high-octane. In protest, women finally took to the streets, calling for equality in their jobs. It was time to pass a women's rights bill to create a more equal society, as the human rights bill was not enough.

Gender equality was expected in the legislature, corporations, and all C-level jobs. Yet, men worked in hazardous conditions for hundreds of years to provide for their families and keep them safe. To put things in perspective for the readers, here are some jobs that have been done exclusively by men since records were kept: combatants, body collectors, miners, labourers,

Upgraditis

railway workers, lumberjacks, fishermen, construction, agriculture, scaffolders, garbage collectors, janitors, truckers, electricity linemen, oil rig workers, machines and equipment maintenance workers, cab drivers, woodworkers, etc. Men sacrificed their lives exploring land, oceans & space, they fought wars, offered their lives to protect the freedom of their countries, and no one asked for equality of outcome in jobs until the air-conditioned office with comfy chairs and coffee machines were invented. However, I noted that no one demanded equality in brick layering, mining, oil rig, construction jobs which surprised me.

Why does it matter whether someone you work with is a guy or a girl? Why is society so obsessed with what is inside of someone's pants? It should only be an issue in private spaces such as bedrooms or toilets, not in boardrooms.

Upgraditis

Instead, there is a growing obsession with establishing an unhealthy environment where private parts influence everything from politics to jobs to sports to entertainment. Organisations recognise people based on their gender, not their intelligence, capability, or competence. Gender is only relevant in specific interactions; the brain is crucial in other areas of life.

The world is on an equality binge - they want to make males and females equal; if they are equal, why did nature create differentiation? Maybe mother nature wants us to take separate paths.

Some people want to erase the difference between genders by indoctrinating women on equality; so, women can start acting like men because the only way to succeed in this world is to be like a man. Trust me, ladies, you don't want to be like a man. Men are messed up.

Most people in jails are men.

Most people who commit suicide are men.

Most people who commit violence are men.

Most people who are victims of violence are men.

Most people who are addicted are men.

Most people who abuse children are men.

Most people who commit murders are men.

Most people who steal, rob and cheat are men.

Most people who gamble are men.

Most people who start wars are men.

Most people who lost lives exploring are men.

Most people who die in adventure sports are men.

Most people who devote entire lives working are men.

The fact is that men are stupid.

It is tough to be a woman in the western world. 42% of the women above 40 yrs. of age are on anti-depressants because most of these women competed with men and started doing the same stupid things that a man does. They are creating this stress in their lives to earn a few more dollars than another man.

God was almost finished creating humanity when he realised he had two spare parts left. Unfortunately, he couldn't decide how to divide them equally between Adam and Eve, so he decided to ask them. He told them that one of the things he had left was the ability for the owner to pee while standing. "It's a handy object," God said, "and I was wondering if any of you had a preference for it."

Adam, on the other hand, jumped up and down and pleaded, "Please, please, please give it to me! That's something I'd love to be able to do! It appears to be precisely what a man should have. Please! Please give it to me!" He went on and on like a thrilled young child. Eve simply laughed and told God that he may have it if Adam desired it so desperately. So, God granted Adam the ability to pee while standing. Adam was so delighted that he just started whizzing around - first on the side of a rock, then he scribbled his name in the sand, and then he tried to hit a tree ten feet away.

God and Eve were amused as they watched him, and God said to Eve, "Well, I guess you are kind of stuck with the last thing I have left."

"What is it called?" Eve inquired.

"Brains," God said.

As I already stated, men are stupid. Women are already superior to men. Women live longer and are less prone to diseases, and you are emotionally and genetically stronger. Women are better learners than men; they are more organised and attentive. Women have a higher IQ than men.

Feminine and masculine have their place in the world. If you destroy the feminine in society, you will genuinely enslave the women. So why do we need to do social engineering on civilisation to make everyone equal? Women should have the freedom to choose on what they want to do. Generally, women are not interested in being plumbers, civil or mechanical engineers or IT programmers. So, let's respect their choice and not force a 50% policy across the board.

In ancient cultures around the world, certain things were done in the society to protect the women of the tribe; as the world progressed, many of these practices became discriminatory and took an ugly shape - we should question those ancient practices and remove them from society, so there is equal opportunity for men and women on things they choose to do.

People misunderstood equality; instead of supporting equality of opportunity, we started supporting equality of outcome.

Upgraditis

Most groups protesting today for equality are asking for equality of outcome, which is a dangerous thing for the future of our civilisation.

Equality of outcome will lead to a society where all fingers are equal. The culture will lack the grip or sensitivity to build the tools to progress. If you want every man or woman to be equal, you will destroy humanity.

Humans are not meant to be equal; instead, machines are made equal.

The grass grows unequally under the sun, and the lawnmower makes the grass equal. Some people act like the sun and grow things, and some people like lawnmowers; they make things equal. The choice is yours

MODERN SLAVERY

Upgraditis

In the last 300 years, we've heard numerous tales about feral kids. In 1975, a 14/15-year-old boy was found in the jungle of Uttar Pradesh; he was raised by wolves. The kids did not possess any human skills, and it was pretty evident that he had spent his entire life with the pack of wolves. He couldn't even get up on two legs because he had never learnt to do that. Yes, we learn or are made to learn; walking on two legs is not natural. We are the only species on earth that always walks with two legs. All other species are evolved to use four limbs. So, walking on two feet is a skill we learn.

Because our forefathers realised that walking on two legs saves energy, we actually burn fewer calories. We figured out this skill when food was scarce. Nature evolved our bodies so we could walk using 4 limbs; at some point, we made a trade-off with nature. Unfortunately, we screwed up the system by walking on two legs. We have disrupted the natural gravitational equilibrium by walking on two legs, whereas other species use all four limbs, coordinated and parallel to the gravitational forces of this planet. But when our forefathers began walking on two legs to save energy, our heart, lungs, and immune systems started to get weaker. The blood must now flow upward, making

Upgraditis

the lungs and heart work much harder than necessary. We are constantly battling gravity by walking upright.

So, this kid couldn't walk on two legs; he had to walk on all four limbs, like wolves. He also ate uncooked meat like wolves. He was practically a wolf in human form, and even eight strong men would struggle to restrain him. He may bite or take some of their flesh. He was a wild creature, not a human.

Then there was an attempt to educate this young guy; he needed to be taught how to speak and write. Also, all kinds of therapies and solutions were provided to him for 6 months, and he could hardly stand on his two feet, and a small gap would send him back to his four, since standing on two was so tricky. His human educators had no idea of the fun of using all fours, as they were standing on their two and suffering.

Rama was the name given to this kid. They'd had enough of educating him, and all he knew and could say before he died was Rama.

He died after living with humans for only 18 months. According to the specialists researching him, the possible reason for his death was the training crush he was given to make him civilised. He was not human, in fact, a child of a wild animal.

Upgraditis

If the education process killed a wolf in human form, what would it be to human kids? This also demonstrates how much of a child's life may be depleted by forcing them to go to the classroom every day and subjecting them to a training crush method. In doing so, we take away their joy and their wildness. That is the crux of the problem in the educational system.

Human kids are like a seed; we are a possibility. A dog is born as a dog and must remain thus throughout its existence. Humans are not born as men or women; we may grow or may not grow. Other creatures do not have a future; only humans do.

> *All animals are born with excellent instincts, whereas humans are born with imperfect faculties. As a result, growth and development are possible.*

Education serves as a link between possibility and reality. The education purchased in ordinary schools, institutes, and campuses is not education. It merely serves to prepare you for a job and a wage.

Another fundamental lie about education has been instilled in you early. The entire educational system is based on lies, such as the idea that anyone can become anything if they receive the appropriate education in that profession. As a result, we psychologically harm children by instilling that they can achieve anything in life if they just study hard enough. Another lie is the educational concept of linearity. It all begins here that you follow a planned route and that if you do things correctly, you will be established for the rest of your life. However, all success stories are non-linear and organic; thus, this is nonsense.

When it comes to human progress, education is the most essential tool. However, this tool is currently being distorted to serve a specific ideology. Because of this, youngsters are being taught what they should think rather than how to think.

> *Unfortunately, two things are broken in the education system: education and the system.*

Schools are relatively new entities in terms of our civilisations written history.

Education 1.0 began thousands of years ago as hunter-gatherers. Kids must master the art of creating and the use of hunting and collecting tools. They did

UPGRADITIS

not, though, have to work long hours, and the work they did was stimulating rather than dull. According to historians, the hunter-gather tribes didn't differentiate between work and play. Through play and discovery, children in hunter-gatherer tribes learnt what they deserved to understand to become fully functional adults. Adults in hunter-gatherer tribes gave kids nearly unrestricted freedom to play and explore independently since they knew that these activities were natural ways to learn. The hunter-gatherer style of existence required a lot of expertise and knowledge but not a lot of hard labor.

Education 2.0 was invented roughly 10,000 years ago when our society first began farming. Agriculture based society helped people produce more food and hence have more kids. Children became involuntary labourers as agriculture developed. Suppressing play and exploration became more prevalent in society. Previously a quality, wilfulness has now become a sin that needs to be beaten out of a kid. Kids had to work on the fields to help nourish their family or work at home to manage their younger siblings. Kids' lives eventually transformed from the free pursuit of play and discovery to the hard work required to aid their families. Slavery and other types of servitude developed under those conditions. Obeyance, suppressing choice, and respect for paymasters were the main lessons taught to kids. A defiant attitude may lead to death. This is how society has conditioned kids for thousands of years. Things started changing in medieval periods as the manufacturing of certain items started. Children's work shifted from fields to dark, overcrowded, filthy, industrious environments. A decent kid was docile, concealing their desire to play and explore to obey their grown-up masters. Thankfully, such education never entirely thrived, as kids were forced to perform hard labor for centuries.

Education 3.0 began when manufacturing advanced and became more mechanised, reducing the necessity for child labor in many areas. Governments around the world started implementing strict child employment laws. Childhood was seen as a period for learning, and classrooms for children were created as schooling systems. The schooling system had numerous proponents and influencers in society. All of these influencers had different ideas about schooling. Industrialists saw education as improving workers' essential reading, writing and punctuality. Politicians saw education as a way to raise patriots and troops. These social influencers agreed and established what kind of education kids should receive. Inculcation, injecting particular ideas and methods of thinking into kids' minds, was their idea. Systematic repetition and assessment for memory became the methods to test learning. With the rise of schooling, learning became a child's work. The same power-assertive practices used to force kids to work in fields and industries inevitably found their way into classrooms. A child's natural tendency is to focus on playing and exploring the environment independently; learning and memorisation make their lives complicated. Like farms and industries, schools were not easily adapted by kids. Most felt they had to be beaten into submission to make kids learn, which went on for a very long time. All forms of discipline were accepted as part of learning. Playing and exploring was the devil in the classroom. During the last century, public education evolved into what we currently known as formal schooling and the number of hours, days, and years of compulsory education have skyrocketed. Gradually, the schools have taken over from farm work, manufacturing jobs, and household duties; kids today spend a six-hour day in the classroom, plus an hour or more of homework and many more hours of courses beyond school. In recent years, education has gotten less unpleasant, but underlying assumptions have not altered. Forced learning is still reminiscent of child labor, and kids don't choose what they want to learn in school. Kids who cannot sit still for classes due to their natural desire to play and explore are drugged with amphetamines and cognitive boosters.

> *As a result of the industrial revolution, educational institutions were established to prepare students for careers in manufacturing, that is why we teach kids to stand in straight and neat lines, that is why we train them to be somewhere else for 8 hours a day with a lunch break. Schools teach kids to sit still for a long time to prepare them to be focused industry workers with high productivity. Schools introduced a grading system, and everyone was incentivised to compete to get an A; Grade A later in life will relate to the product quality they needed to produce in those factories. Times have changed, and we are still making robots for **Industry** through our education system.*

UPGRADITIS

Education systems are a supply industry for societies current industrial needs. Let's suppose a world war starts, the schools will adapt to make everybody a soldier. If everyone was sick, the schools would supply more doctors and nurses. If everyone in society started fighting with each other, the schools would provide more lawyers. Schools are just training you to serve someone else, and you think you are free. The education system enslaves young boys and girls to help a social structure. In education, the trend is not your friend. Parents have a social proclivity to push kids into specific professional courses based on today's demands. Unfortunately, the market is usually not there when you complete your graduation in that domain, and you find yourself driving Uber with substantial financial debt. These establishments suffocated our kids' creativity, transforming them into tedious algorithms. Because it is an archaic system that has outlived its usefulness, the educational system has become obsolete. Nevertheless, a few things have changed in classrooms over 150 years ago; the architecture of thought has remained unchanged, and the educational system professes to prepare kids for their future.

Upgraditis

You are a victim of the education system that just supplies spare parts to the main machine, i.e., Industry. Human kids have become the fuel that fires up this machine.

Sometimes this machine is called the economic engine of civilisation. Rather the goal should be to enhance human ability and intelligence. Education should not be making something for someone; instead, it should teach how to find your full potential. The education system is no longer about people.

Education is meant to make you rich inside. Educating someone doesn't just make them extra knowledgeable; that's an ancient theory of what it means to learn; it's called rudimentary because it's based on fear, on the belief that "if I don't get a good education, I won't be able to sustain." But, on the other hand, it teaches you how to compete, making you want to be better. It's just a way to get ready for a world where everyone is your opponent.

Furthermore, education should equip you to be who you are. Unfortunately, it is preparing you to be a copycat; it teaches you to mimic somebody else. This is a case of willful ignorance. No one has ever been, or will ever be, like you. This is your brilliance: you are one-of-a-kind. Don't be replicas of others. But that's precisely what your so-called schooling is doing: it's making clones and erasing your innovative features.

Learning is not the same as knowing. Unfortunately, knowing has become overly intertwined with learning. A human's ability to learn decreases as his knowledge increases. As a result, kids are more capable of learning than adults. The kid's brilliance is that they operate from a place of not knowing, and this is the essential secret of learning, operating from such a place of not knowing. Always have an open mind and never jump to conclusions. Learning comes to an end when you've reached a conclusion.

To achieve success, we must examine our abilities in the context of our circumstances. Unfortunately, the education system wants everyone to finish high school and go to university, which has led to a fixation on this linear paradigm throughout society. I am not proposing that you do not attend university, but I am stating that not everyone is required.

Good schooling and education may not necessarily indicate intelligence, merit, or human worth. The scientific community agrees that genetics plays a significant role in determining I.Q. in children, rather than shared settings such as schools. When children are given I.Q. tests at the ages of 6, 12, and 18, there is a clear correlation that I.Q. does not change due to their education. It is sad to see 4-5-year-old kids being interviewed for Kindergarten, kids sitting in front of a panel and trying to impress them with their resumes on achievements in the last 48 months on this planet. Many schools are introducing entrance tests for Kindergarten; this is child abuse.

> *Education is the process of drawing out what is already within you, much like drawing water out of a well. Contradictory to this, everything is being poured into you. Literature, economics, physics, and math's are all being poured into you at an increasing rate.*

Your academic institutions are sites where you are stuffed full of information in your brain. Real education will be about bringing out what is buried within you, discovering it, revealing it, and illuminating you from within. Conditioning and the educational process we go through diminish consciousness.

UPGRADITIS

An insomniac boxer sought medical attention from a doctor to alleviate his symptoms. Mild sedation has been attempted before, but it did not appear to be effective. So rather than prescribing a more powerful medication, the doctor suggested that the patient try a vintage cure before turning to a more modern approach.

Doctor: "You might think it's ridiculous, yet it truly works. Try to become entirely comfortable before counting to a 100 with your eyes closed".

The boxer returned a few days later and told the doctor, "Doctor, I'm not up to it." Each and every time I begin counting, I jump up at the count of 9.

I refer to this as education or conditioning; it absorbs your conscious awareness.

·········· ● ·············

You think you got an education in the school you attended for 14 years, think again, how much of that you use daily, monthly, annually, or never. Schools are day cares so kids can stay in a building while the parents can go and work somewhere. High schools and colleges are prisons for many; boys would overrun society and cause a lot of havoc on the streets if not appropriately controlled. The medieval universities and colleges had inward-facing guard towers to create a curfew-like environment so teenage males didn't run wild. These old schools and universities come from a time when knowledge was rare and books were rare, violence was prevalent in the society, and no self-guided learning was possible as the knowledge was not widely distributed. So, schools became the byproducts of these circumstances. Now we have the internet if we desire to learn anything, we can self-learn from the finest minds on this planet for free. You can attend the lectures of professors of Harvard, Stanford, and Yale. Learning is infinite in today's society.

The education system is redundant for self-motivated and self-learners, the self-starters. The education system for the majority is to babysit their kids while they make money; it is excellent for socialisation as kids are around other kids but not for learning. So, learning should be about learning only basic principles in all fields and learning them very well. Life is all about applying basic principles effectively. Advanced stuff should be optional for people interested in taking the next step. Instead, the schools taught calculus to kids struggling to understand the basics of mathematics.

There is another issue, schools teach all irrelevant things that you will never use and completely ignore the important stuff in life.

UPGRADITIS

Schools are good in teaching:

- How to find X.
- Mathematical theorems.
- Laws of thermodynamics.
- Newtown's laws of motion.
- Organic chemistry.
- Calculus etc.

I wish schools taught me:

- How to manage my emotions.
- How to build relationships.
- How to invest and make money.
- How to cook, which is a critical survival skill.
- How to stay positive.
- How to look after my mental health.
- How to keep my body fit.
- How to be calmer.
- How to think.
- How to negotiate.
- How to start a company.

Upgraditis

Since the school system is an over-leveraged business plan that is oblivious to the goals and abilities of young children, this problem will be challenging to resolve. Degrees have suddenly become worthless in the eyes of employers. They are like the taxi plates, which are now essentially useless. A degree used to be sufficient proof of employment, but nowadays, highly educated youngsters drive Uber taxis; their star rating on Uber has effectively replaced their resumes.

Religious education is the lowest form of education that a person can obtain. Yet, until recently, every culture has worked to brainwash every child. Answers are provided to the child before they can ask questions. Do you see how ridiculous it is? You offer an answer to a child who has not asked the question. The child is powerless to do anything. A child naturally believes in the mother, father, and preacher whom his father and mother both trusts. The phenomena of doubt haven't yet manifested themselves. You must sharpen your skeptical energies so that you can see past the nonsense and ask questions that no one can answer.

Upgraditis

The primary purpose of education should be to broaden the horizons of human beings, but this is not occurring at the present time, according to experts. In becoming more educated, people are losing their ability to get along with other individuals. This is the nature of human intellect: the better informed you are, the more alienated you will become; today's education is solely based on intellect.

It is common for people to make a mistake in understanding the difference between intelligence and intellect. If you are familiar with all of the topics covered by Wikipedia, you are considered intellectual. If you can put that information to create something, you are intelligent. Regrettably, our educational system merely develops intellect rather than intelligence; as a result, our educational system produces factory workers rather than geniuses.

Upgraditis

Similarly, to how we must strip-mine the planet for specific elements and materials, our educational system has strip-mined our minds for specific talent and creativity. It will be of no use to us in the future.

We must reconsider the underlying foundations on which we base our decision to educate our children. Or else, we will raise kids who derive no enjoyment from their profession; they will bear it for five days and then look forwards to the weekend. Education must bring everyone together with your passions, not separate them from their natural abilities. Talent is similar to a natural resource in that it is hidden deep within each one of us. We have to go out and look for it, just as natural resources aren't just lying there on the surface waiting to be discovered. The educational system must create the conditions in which this type of ability can manifest itself.

It's only a question of degree among a lethal and a medicinal dose of strychnine. The poison can act as a medicine when given in small doses, but the same treatment can be lethal when given in larger doses. It becomes toxic at some point and ceases to be medication.

Upgraditis

Humans can no longer serve education in the same way we used to because of the rapid pace of change. Previously, people were coached in memorisation. Up until now, education has focused primarily on memory rather than intelligence. The earlier generations passed on all of its information to the new generation, which was expected to memorise it. As a result, individuals with good memories were considered intelligent. Unfortunately, that isn't always the case. For example, Albert Einstein had a terrible memory. There have been individuals with extraordinary memories but lacked intelligence. In your case, memory is a mechanical process. Consciousness is intelligence. Memory is a part of your brain, and intelligence is a part of your spirit. The body is responsible for memory, but you are responsible for intelligence. Intelligence must now be taught since change is so rapid that memorisation will no longer suffice. It is already out of date by the time you memorise something. And that is precisely what is happening: education is failing, institutions are failing because they are still clinging to the old ways of doing things.

Keep your children out of an industrial education paradigm, a manufacturing model built on linearity and batching people based on general traits, which is not what you want for your children.

Upgraditis

> *Instead, choose a paradigm that is more founded on gardening principles. You must realise that human education is not a mechanical process; it is organic, and you cannot predict how your children will develop. As a gardener, all you can do is establish the conditions that will allow them to begin to thrive as quickly as possible.*

Not only does your child require more inspiration, but they also require more play and exploration rather than merely information.

FINDING LOVE

Upgraditis

When I was growing up, I watched Bollywood movies; during the 1980s and 1990s, practically every Bollywood film released had the same love plot-line. However, sadly, those films were romantic and predictable in their plots. First, two romantically challenged characters will meet and fall in love. Then, they encounter a challenge that separates them; towards the climax, they will eventually come back together and be wrapped in each other's arms.

Each of the folks I grew up with was also raised on these imaginary love stories filled with singing and dancing. But, unfortunately, neither of these scenarios came near to the paths of real-life love stories that I had personally experienced. Because of these films, we have a distorted view of love and romance.

As a result of globalisation and the cable television boom in India, I was introduced to Hollywood in the 1990s. I could see that Hollywood was taking love stories to a whole new level. Hollywood was responsible for inflating people's expectations of love; this was compounded by television and romance novels.

The screen was reframing lust as love and serving this bullshit to the masses in a glamorous way. There were many millions of unhappy couples as a result. Because the romantic storylines they'd seen on screen didn't match what they'd experienced in their own homes.

The movies sparked a widespread craze about love. But, unfortunately, the following lies about love were peddled to you by the film and television, and you fell for them. You've lived with it for years, and you're probably still living with it:

LOVE AT FIRST SIGHT:

In movies, this notion is used only when it is suitable for the film's timeline. The film is just a couple of hours long, and we need to fit in all the other characters and events in that time. As a result, Cinema created falling in love at first sight. Attraction or lust, at first sight, is the real-life equivalents of this concept.

THEY LIVED HAPPILY EVER AFTER:

As soon as the movie is completed, the audience is led to assume that the imaginary couple has now been married for a long term and will live happily ever after. Believe me, when I say that this is far from reality - the ultimate shit show begins immediately later, and the truth is not as seamless as it appears in the movies. People grow in different ways; hence the phrase "they live happily ever after" does not persist indefinitely.

THE ONE:

Myths like there is a soul mate, "the one" who is solely for you, and that your life's mission is to discover them are also created by movies. When it comes to marriage, people who often believe in the soul mate myth have a highly problematic relationship; their relationships are complicated. They cannot collaborate because they do not get that love is participatory. This is a harmful concept because it may lead people to believe their love lives are out of their hands.

OPPOSITES ATTRACT:

Films like Titanic and Pretty Woman portray this false reality. The discrepancies in the riches and lifestyle of a character are no match for their unflattering characteristics. Once you've been married for a while, you'll realise that the more unlike the daily rituals and tastes of two people are, the less probable it is that they will be able to stay together indefinitely and happily. People with significantly divergent worldviews are unlikely to be harmonious with one another.

LOVE CAN CHANGE PEOPLE:

The character of Belle from the film Beauty and the Beast strives to soften the beast's demeanour through unconditional love. Bullshit. In real life, she would have resigned after becoming frustrated. In a bad relationship, demonstrating thoughtfulness and reliance exposes the fixer to the possibility of relationship abuse.

WITH LOVE, WE WILL CONQUER ALL:

Love is helpless in the face of external forces; it cannot cure illness, avert bankruptcy, prevent people from dying, or even put food on the table for their families. In real life, when long-term unromantic circumstances arise, they usually cause damage to even the most committed of couples' relationships.

"I LOVE YOU" MANTRA:

As movies and TV portrays couples with non-stop over the top romantic moments, where couples are consumed in expressing their love verbally to each other. But love is not a series of grand gestures; it is more like a succession of small gestures. It merely happens while you're having a pleasant conversation with a companion. The most loveable times in your real-life relationships will be the silent ones, when you're just hanging out, cooking along, or laughing together at silly jokes. Major declarations of love and extravagant gestures do not constitute a genuine relationship; this is nonsense that society feeds you while you are growing up.

YOU SACRIFICE INCREDIBLE OPPORTUNITIES FOR LOVE:

I've seen how characters in movies or television shows always seem to pass up excellent opportunities. If someone truly cared about you in real life, they would not expect you to give up so much of yourself.

⋯⋯••••••●•••••••⋯⋯

Young people's perceptions of love are distorted by television and movies, which instils incorrect perspectives and unrealistic expectations in their minds. Individuals form relationships within a comfortable, profitable, or adventurous framework based on their unique physical, emotional, and social demands, which vary from person to person. The most effective technique to meet their needs is to repeat the phrase "I love you" repeatedly, to try to obtain what you desire by communicating your desires verbally to others.

Movies program your mind to say, "I cannot live without you" it is like saying, "I cannot walk without

Upgraditis

these crutches". Over time the conditioning has made you believe that you cannot walk without those crutches.

> *When your hormones take over your intelligence, you may believe that you have fallen in love with someone. Usually, the tingling sensation you get in your body when you see your crush is generated by your common sense exiting your body and mind.*

That is why it is referred to as "falling in love," because you must first fall to be hurt afterwards. These hormones are produced by nature, pushing you towards someone even if you are not in love with them. However, your genes are only concerned with one thing: reproducing as many copies of themselves as possible. This is the genuine essence of the obsessive love that you may be experiencing now. You mistake the chemical urge that has been established in your body for love. Upon completion of the chemical reaction, many of you would question why you are in this relationship in the first place with this idiot. Hollywood's love story feeds you are nothing more than the chemistry established by your own physical body.

Upgraditis

The cornerstone of life is based on sexuality. It is at the very heart of our being, and our lives are always moving in that direction. Every component of life works together to ensure the survival and growth of the entire system of living things. Sexuality is undoubtedly the most crucial component since life is sustained and struggles for the collective state of existence. We need and seek more than just physical and sexual contact to be completely human. We're looking for a deeper level of connection and understanding. However, while we are all aware of this and aspire to achieve our conscious aims of harmony and love, the physical survival force of sex is actively working to prevent us from achieving these objectives.

If we break down our sexuality into its constituent parts, we can categorise its objectives into two groups. Love and lust are two different things. Our intended purpose is to be in love with one another. And then there's lust, which is our biological unconscious. Of course, we want to meet the needs of both, and we can. However, only if a specific order and procedure are followed. Otherwise, we will be continually bouncing between the two, failing to attain either goal in its entirety.

Lust is more easily attained than love; lust is hollow if not accompanied by love. Lust is a needy and greedy creature. It demands our complete attention and is concerned with nothing else than itself. When we pursue lust, we are compelled to put love aside. When we give in to lust, we find ourselves attracted to everyone and, as a result, to no one in particular. We will never find love through lust. We may pretend that we have, but we would be deluding ourselves in the process. Although lust usually always indicates the presence of feelings of love, it does not necessarily guarantee them.

Lust is a never-ending cycle of anticipation, action, pleasure, regret, and repetition. Of course, we want to find love at some point throughout this cycle as well. But it isn't there, is it? When it comes to love and human goals, lust has no interest. When people confuse lust with love, they end up causing a lot of problems in their relationships and marriages.

So, what is love?

Love is an internal state; it is how you feel inside. Therefore, you must learn to generate it the same way a power plant does; it does not obtain energy from somewhere; instead, it creates energy. When you look at everything through the lens of love, the entire world will become beautiful, and you will have beautiful experiences.

The concept of love is straightforward: it is not intended to cause pain. On the contrary, we enjoy being loved so much because it brings us to a state of blissfulness. Love is not the goal; blissfulness is the goal, and love serves as a vehicle to carry one to a blissful state.

Young people are infatuated with the concept of falling in love because it transports them to their desired destination, i.e., a favourable condition, for some time, which they find appealing. They begin to believe that love is a favourable condition when, in fact, it is the emotional currency that is exchanged for blissfulness. Young brains don't have many solutions for putting their minds and bodies in a joyful state; the only mechanism they come across is love, and as a result, they get obsessed with the concept of love. As they grow older, they will discover new and exciting ways to enjoy blissful experiences, and the urge to be continually loved will gradually fade away.

Upgraditis

If you are exclusively interested in sensory pleasures or physical attraction as a means of finding happiness, you are likely to be quite selective about the people whom you choose to love in your life.

Love is not something you do with someone; love is how you are. You are just using the other person as an excuse to open this state of blissfulness.

If emotions have different tastes, then love certainly has the sugary taste; it is a sweet emotion. Love is just the sweetness of your feeling; if you need other people in your life to trigger it, then you are walking with crutches.

Love comes in hierarchies as well.

The lowest kind of love that you will experience is love for power. When love is infected by the idea of controlling others or becoming powerful, then it takes the shape of politics. Politics can happen between any two individuals in a relationship. People with an addiction to power enjoy love for dominations and control. So many people love their dogs, cats, birds, cars, horses, and machines; because you can control them quickly, and they don't try to dominate you. People find themselves in this lowest form of Love because Love for other humans has resulted in a conflict and has inflicted so much pain in their lives. Nothing is wrong with you if you love this way.

The highest form of love a human can experience is when love becomes your state of existence. This kind of love doesn't demand anything in return, like a mother's love for their child.

Love is breath, and it is more powerful than you can fathom. However, you are not required to possess it. It can only be possessed by you if you allow yourself to be possessed by it. The ego wants to control just about everything, so you become anxious about anything you cannot control. Possessiveness, the desire to own, has killed the ability to love. Don't think about what you own. Instead, think about being owned. It means to be possessed that you let yourself be owned by something bigger than you. People have trouble with love because they don't have this ability. Therefore, most people can't love.

If you have been a love gypsy all your life and have hopped from one relationship to another in search of true love, then let me tell you that the common denominator in all those failed relationships is you. Maybe you are still looking for the Hollywood love that happens on the screen; if you haven't found it, you will never. As what you are searching for in other people is within, you never learnt how to generate it.

> *Love, in many cases, is like beggars begging from beggars; you want to give something that you don't have, and you are asking for something that the other person doesn't possess.*

True love is like breathing; it is always there with you if you are alive. Love is subjective radiation that you project on all objects and people; the more significant the radiation, the greater is your blissful experience. The bigger the sky of bliss, the larger your wings will get, and you will enjoy every day of your lives.

6
TECHNOLOGY CONNECTS

Upgraditis

In the last century, tobacco firms have used every excuse in the book to hook the public on their lethal products; they advertised smoking as a way to live a wealthier, more luxurious lifestyle. Cigarette advertising explicitly directed at female consumers first appeared in the 1920s and 1930s in American and European markets. Smoking quickly became a sign of being on par with males, and cigarette companies became a big supporter of the equality movement. Cigarettes became a "torch for freedom" among sophisticated women worldwide.

Tobacco corporations employed doctors and dentists to support their products in the 1940s to alleviate public health worries about the dangers of smoking. Tobacco firms mislead customers with slogans like "Just what the doc ordered" and "More physicians smoke Camels."

Tobacco corporations owned and funded their own TV shows in the 1950s and 1960s and paid A-list celebrities to feature in promotional campaigns. Later, cultural idols like the Marlboro Man lured men with exaggerated ideals of manhood and independence. Professional athletes have even been employed by smokeless tobacco businesses to promote their goods. It was a low-cost, legal, and socially desirable commodity. Cigarettes corporations used cartoon characters like Joe Camel in the 1980s to increase the attractiveness of tobacco to children. Although this tactic has been outlawed, the deceit continues with delicious flavours and brightly coloured smoking products.

Society fed us bullshit about smoking for 80 years. But then, it started becoming quite evident in the 1960s that smoking leads to cardiovascular, lung diseases, including cancers. It nearly took three human generations to determine how these companies destroyed lives by getting us addicted to their products.

Similarly, we are now addicted to technology. We pick up our phones 80 times per day, nearly every 12 minutes. We've been addicted. Nearly one-third of the population feels anxious when separated from their phone. Nomophobia, or the fear of being without one's phone, is becoming more prevalent.

Did I just compare cigarettes with smartphones?

Yes, I did.

Like cigarettes, society tells us that technology and popular applications built on the internet will make lives extraordinary; we will learn more and connect with people better. However, the reality is far different than what is projected and advertised by the big tech or social media companies.

> *When the connectivity bar on our devices is active, we step further away from connecting with humans.*

A majority of grown-ups today have an attention span of a toddler; it is getting increasingly difficult to have good eye contact or deep conversations. So, while people have an extensive friend list on their anti-social networks, in reality, they are friendless. Yes, it should be called the anti-social network because that's what it exactly does.

Today, an average person will spend almost 5 years of their life looking down on their touchscreen phones while losing touch with their lives. I often wonder what the alphabet 'I' stands for in iPhones, iPads etc. Constant virtual interactions are deepening our loneliness. Of course, loneliness existed long before we could compare follower counts. Loneliness is and has always been a universal human condition. But it's affecting more people, with some anticipating a loneliness epidemic.

UPGRADITIS

Research suggests our relationships with technology shape our sense of loneliness, creating a false sense of connectedness. Unlimited engagement options reduce our tolerance for solitude. Technology can consume our minds and prevent us from noticing the lack of connections in our life. It can also hinder us from reaping the benefits of solitude and dullness. Both, in proportion, can foster identity, inventiveness, and a new respect for essential bonds.

When mirrors became accessible in the late nineteenth century, they caused people to worry about how they presented to others in a far more conscious manner than they had previously. Later, the camera opened up photography to anyone, the ability to show themselves in photographs while massively increasing their degrees of self-criticism. Finally, these adverse effects of self-portrayal became quite evident when social media was invented.

The radio, introduced in the 1920s and 1930s, was a device that would instantly replace solitude with sounds with the twist of a knob. It was the first time you could beam down a musician to your living room. It was more difficult to feel alone when the entire family was assembled in the living room, listening to the radio. With the invention of smartphones, the loneliness score of humanity skyrocketed; yes, we became more connected but are we really connecting? Did we become more connected but without any real connections? But society told us that technology connects; instead, it makes us isolated.

•••••••• • •••••••

The arms race was intense in the years leading up to World War II and throughout the war. Nazi scientists had a significant advantage in inventing novel methods of wreaking havoc. A unique ability to think outside the box and come up with lethal advancements was exhibited by the Nazis, which was further bolstered by their ability to scale concepts into practical designs and then mass produce them on a massive scale. Helicopters, cruise missiles, dive bombers, space planes, rockets, space weapons, and the world's most lethal tanks were all developed by the Nazis during World War II. They were only a few steps away from developing the atomic bomb; they were also working on anti-gravity planes and space weapons at the time. Hitler and his associates adopted the agile paradigm of technology innovation. Hitler dispatched his innovation project managers worldwide in search of new and innovative ideas to implement. There are accounts of Nazi scientists travelling to Antarctica to do experiments. Nazis travelled to India to translate Vedas, the ancient books. Nazis also travelled to tribal and primitive areas to study Voodoo and black magic; Hitler was a firm believer in the fail-fast approach.

Consider the possibility of Nazis inventing the internet and the devices that run several world wide web applications. What would have transpired if this had happened? It will be a remarkable hypothetical thought experiment that allows us to comprehend what Hitler might have done if he and his military had access to today's internet technologies and intelligent devices. As far as I can guess, Hitler would have weaponised any sort of technology available to him; he might even have repurposed internet technology into some form of weapon of mass destruction. In addition, Hitler could have turned the internet into a dangerous force to eliminate all enemy nations' confidence, guaranteeing that these nations did not offer any opposition to the Nazi armies on their borders.

So, let's go a little more into this hypothetical thought experiment to see where it leads. But first, let's envision what a Nazi weapon development roadmap fueled by the internet would look like. After all, Hitler was the world's most evil supervillain.

Probably, the first product that Nazi technology enterprise would have built would have been the nPad, that is Nazi Pad; just like Apple's iPad, the nPad would have been a more rudimentary version. I can imagine Hitler offering the nPad as a capitalist, marketing these devices worldwide and claiming that it will make everybody's lives better due to their purchase. But, of course, if marketing companies today bend the truth to sell their products while misrepresenting them, the Nazi marketing department would have had little trouble distorting the truth and pushing misleading advertisements.

nPad in those times would have been the most futuristic concept that's never been thought of by any other invader, commander, king, or queen, military general or dictator in the history of the world. This nPad would have given the Nazi forces boundless power and would serve as a shortcut to world dominance. Hitler would have planned to produce this device and transport it to every country on the planet, collecting revenue in the process. This nPad would have been appropriate for people of all ages, from toddlers to those on their deathbeds.

Upgraditis

Kids would have loved this device, and they can play engaging games, watch videos, and even build a virtual world with virtual relationships for themselves. These devices will become the new babysitter. If you want your toddlers to shut up and sit in one place, hand them the device and leave the room. Once you are back, your toddler will not have moved or blinked, as the toddler is so engaged in watching silly cat videos. It will be so addictive for the toddlers that they will never find books engaging or find storytelling engaging. Their brain circuit will be trained for constant engagement, and the brain's reward mechanism will look for continuous dopamine slingshots. Now, these toddlers will think that this is a part of their body and show withdrawal symptoms when the device is not around. These toddlers will develop introverted personalities and find human contact uncomfortable when they grow up; they will get addicted to endless scrolls of cat videos and entertaining content and create a deep bond with the laughter and comfort that comes with zero effort. This toddler will slowly crave this nPad just like a baby that craves mothers' milk and warmth.

For grown-up kids, nPad will be a faithful companion. They will take it everywhere, trust it, and spend 4-8 hours a day with it. They will sit in front of it for hours and play games, endless pursuits to achieve nothing but a dopamine slingshot. They will take it to dinner tables, restaurants, and every social event their parents attend. Now the engaging dinner table conversations will be replaced by kids watching other kids play video games. The dinner table will no longer be a place where parents did excellent storytelling and engaged kids with tales of adventure.

With this new weaponised technology, Hitler would kill the sense of adventure in all the kids; now, these kids will not want to leave their homes and stay in their rooms pushing buttons on this nPad. They will be acutely anxious about real life when they grow up as they lack experience and exposure to life's challenges. These kids will not have the courage or a desire for real-world adventure - They will not become explorers of the natural world; instead, their experiences will be different, like Crossy Road or Flappy bird or Minecraft. These kids will not find joy in climbing a mountain, long walks, discovering new places, sitting, and discussing ideas or looking into someone's eyes and feeling what they feel. Instead, their joy will come from this nPad. With this nPad, Hitler would possibly cripple the sense of adventure and real-world courage in kids to become great leaders.

Teenagers will use nPad, and Hitler would use it to cripple them intellectually and make them woke. So, they start fighting the system they are a part of and use the energy and focus for divisive politics. Hitler would make politics like a sport, so each side cheers for their team. As propaganda will be delivered through this nPad, these kids already trust this device and remember it's part of their bodies. Hitler would have converted all teenagers into screenagers.

Hitler would have also planned to destroy the minds and bodies of men who would usually give Nazi's forces resistance in the Wars. Hitler would also make porn and micro-content apps, where men can sit and watch attractive women. These men will get dissatisfied with their wives and girlfriends and lose interest in their relationships. Why would a man find his wife attractive if he can experience an incredible blood rush in his body if a supermodel takes her clothes off just for him, even though she is on the other side of the nPad? This man addicted to pleasure will have the superpower to choose or change the supermodel with a single tap on the nPad, and the options will be infinite. This fully grown man will find real sex undesirable because his wife or girlfriend is not as desirable as the buffet of supermodels his brain likes. Slowly, these men will start having fewer kids and will be more miserable in their married lives as the reality is not as great as what the brain experiences on nPad. Fewer kids mean fewer people to fight the enemy, and sad men are less motivated to do anything new.

Aged men will not have many people around them as everyone in their family will be glued to the nPad. So, they will have no one to share their wisdom with. Eventually, they will also fall victim to the news propaganda and derive pleasure from this nPad.

If we take a step back and look at this hypothetical experiment, Hitler's master plan was to weaponise technology to cripple intellect, adventure, courage, social structure, and the sense of reality for all the enemy nations. So, a generation later, he can walk over their borders without resistance.

Do you know what the sad part of this story is?

What Hitler would have done with the enemy nations; you are doing it to your kids.

Upgraditis

The use of social media, primarily through phones, appears to impair our capability to manage and balance time, emotion, and focus, resulting in lifestyle modification and behavioural impairments. We should avoid social nibbling. It is defined as looking through accounts, viewing everyone's status updates, and viewing everyone's comments and replies without participating in any of the activities involved. At the moment, social nibbling may appear to be a form of social engagement, and you may momentarily ignore your own feelings of isolation while you're doing it.

> *The problem is that just as fast food makes you feel full and hollow later, social nibbling just results in lost time and more loneliness than you started with.*

Furthermore, you will not develop a lasting relationship with anyone until you talk about genuine concerns and share real troubles with them.

Internet addiction and computer games influence morale, motivation, memory, and other aspects of psychological functioning. The suicide rate in America for 12 to 34 years has risen sharply since 2013. Since 2008, the birth rate in the United States has been declining, while occurrences of young adult sexual dysfunction due to massive internet pornography consumption have increased.

> *Generation Z is the loneliest generation*
> *and appears worse than older generations.*
> *The freshest and most connected generation*
> *appears to be in the worse shape.*

There is a less desire for freedom; less willingness to take risks; boys more fixated with video games and girls more focused on social media; depression and anxiety associated with loneliness; digital isolation; neglect of friends and family; constant comparison with others' digital lives. The World Health Organisation formally acknowledged technology addiction altering motivation, memory, and other aspects of psychological functioning.

Society tells us technology is fantastic and technology transforms lives. But unfortunately, most people today are bought into this bullshit narrative and herd mentality. Yes, razor blades and knives are fantastic and transform people's lives in surgery, cooking, hunting & shaving, but do you hand them out to your young children?

Upgraditis

Suddenly, this device in your pocket designed to serve you as a slave became your master. You got addicted, your kids got addicted, your wife got addicted, and this is intellectually and morally crippling your future.

This is what Hitler wanted. So, Hitler says, 'Thank you.'

I know you have a lot of screens in your home, probably three screens per person. Let's say there was a timer that recorded every unnecessary moment wasted by humanity in front of the screen; what would that number look like for society? Let try to calculate the number with napkin math's.

Seven billion people in the world.

Let's assume everyone on this planet wastes one hour a day doing something completely useless while staring at a screen. I am totally reasonable here, and I have seen 6 hours of daily Instagram usage on some phones. This equates to 7 Billion hours lost every day, watching videos on TikTok or making a pigeon cross the road in the game or scrolling through propaganda on your favourite social media platform.

Seven Billion hours equate to 100,000 human lifetimes a day.

Upgraditis

Every day, the smartphone in your pocket generates a meaningless information tsunami that ends the lives of 100,000 people.

That's a hundred thousand human lives a day that could have been spent telling your loved one how much you care.

To put it another way, that's one hundred thousand human lives a day that could be spent inventing something new, doing good, or simply talking to someone you care about.

A hundred thousand human lives are squandered every day that could have been spent to care for mental or physical health.

Every day, we waste a hundred thousand human lives that could have been spent cooking delicious cuisine for our loved ones.

Just imagine if humans didn't destroy 100,000 humans' lives every day for the last 20 years - we would have flying cars by now, we would have cured cancer and all the diseases. But, instead, these screens became the cancer of society. This was Hitler's vision for enemy nations.

Upgraditis

Now you are going to argue how technology has made life remarkable. Yes, I agree it did. But be aware of the implications of a 5-year-old kid spending the most time with video games, Netflix & YouTube. The consequences we see as a society are Sleep deprivation, physical & mental strain, weak eyes and body, obesity, chronic health conditions, loss of cognitive ability, declining conversational competence, low self-esteem, low confidence, depression, and anxiety about real-world issues, loss of interest in life, loss of relationships, failure of self-control, loneliness, communication challenges and the list goes on.

> *We have developed smart cows who produce tremendous amounts of milk but are otherwise significantly inferior to their wild counterparts in temperament and overall health. Similarly, in the process of making smart kids, we are training the next generation to be a commodity that produces a large amount of data for tech companies.*

Yes, they produce a lot of data, but these kids lack agility, resourcefulness, motivation, and courage. As a result, we may wind up with degraded humans who use improved computers to wreak havoc on themselves and the rest of humanity if we do not take precautionary measures now.

Our desire for always being engaged and connected comes at a cost. That trade-off is empathy and creativity. The brain areas responsible for creativity and empathy are only lit up in an fMRI scan when the subject observed is not doing anything. So, creativity and empathy are only generated in our brains when we are bored. However, the moment you start doing an activity, mental or physical, the neural activity in those areas die down completely. Master the art of sitting still and doing nothing.

Unfortunately, our bizarre obsession with our smartphones simultaneously kills our capacity to be bored and prohibits us from ever actually being delighted. As a result, we're rendering ourselves more susceptible to boredom by constantly reaching for our phones, which prevents us from letting our minds roam and solving our own boredom issues. When standing in line at the supermarket, meeting at work, or in a reception area, avoid the temptation to scroll. Your cognition, mood, and productivity may increase due to boredom.

Upgraditis

There are various ways to generate a sense of boredom, such as picking an activity that needs little or no focus, like walking a known path, swimming laps, or even just sitting with your eyes closed. During this timeframe, it is indeed critical to turn off any electronics. Boredom can provide us with a short vacation from the constant barrage of messages, emails and social networking notifications that bombard our minds with data and stimuli daily. We need to learn how to step away from these pressures long enough to enjoy the perks of boredom. Boredom takes you to unique places; even this book came out of the boredom I experienced during the COVID lockdowns.

Boredom is beautiful; master the art of boredom.

Make sure you teach your kids to get bored; this will boost their creativity. Have you ever seen a poet, artist, or author with a screen in their hand while creating something new? Instead, they turn to nature, isolate themselves, lock themselves in a room, and get bored. The moment your brain is bored, creative solutions will come automatically.

UPGRADITIS

Don't give these devices to your young kids, instead help them create exciting adventures outside the house; they need to run, explore, climb trees, chase butterflies, and make real friends that genuinely care about them. Their bodies need to be challenged every day to grow to their full potential as a healthy mind lives in a healthy body.

Our obsession with technology has taken us into unexplored terrain. We are not yet aware of the extent of the damage, but it interferes with our capacity to communicate and connect more deeply. For example, the act of smoking was considered seductive, enjoyable, socially active, so everyone did it. Perhaps, with time, we will come to recognise the hazards of technology and better govern how we, and our kids, interact with technology.

You may be the Elephant here; The Elephant man could be the device in your pocket. You are restricted with an invisible chain; you feel compelled to fill the empty time with endless scrolling. As a result, you waste time; that time wasted was called life, which will only happen once. This universe waited 13.7 billion years so you could be born; use that opportunity. Use that time to sit still, get bored and observe life. Trust me; you will be more creative, innovative, calm, and well connected with others.

PERFECTLY FLAWED

UPGRADITIS

There was a time in my life when I used to punish myself and others around me because I was a perfectionist, thus making this world a more miserable place to live. My demands were unrealistic; I was harsh on myself and others. Despite everything, I am no longer a fool; I have effectively removed the perfectionist app from my consciousness.

According to the statistics, perfectionists are less prone to suicide than others. This is most likely because perfectionists continually keep rewriting their suicide notes. After all, nothing is ever perfect.

It must be killing them.

Birds of similar feathers flock together, so as I grew up, I became friends with other idiots who were perfectionists. I observed that perfectionism was more familiar with kids whose parents punished them for mistakes. But, of course, I could be wrong, as my data is not perfect these days.

I recall a talented childhood friend who was disappointed when he did not receive a perfect mark in mathematics. His father worked as a maths educator somewhere else and insisted on perfection in mathematics because the 90s were not good enough for him. He believed that his father would only love him if he received a perfect score, i.e., 100 in mathematics. Consequently, I sat by and watched him battle psychologically for years, semester after semester chasing perfection in exchange for love. Unfortunately, he was also after perfection in other areas of his life, such as writing, reading, dressing, athletics, etc.

He was like Sisyphus from Greek mythology.

Sisyphus was the King of Ephyra. Zeus punished him and was forced to roll a massive rock uphill to roll down every time he reached the peak. He repeated that action for eternity. Through the classical influence on modern culture, laborious and futile tasks are described as Sisyphean. Perfection is Sisyphean; it can never be achieved. Society conditions us to push a massive rock uphill to prove that we are not flawed and worthy. Society doesn't tell us that once we are about to reach the peak, we will be forced down again to a fresh lowland of shame in another domain so we can start climbing repeatedly.

Perfection can't be achieved; instead, we put ourselves in a vicious circle of self-defeat.

Upgraditis

Many of us were brought up to be perfectionists by our society, which educated us that perfection was terrific quality. When I was growing up, I watched interviews with affluent and famous people, and they used to brag about their perfectionism. As a result of seeing these interviews with great performers, musicians, and even technologists such as Steve Jobs, I believe that striving for perfection will lead to greatness and that this pursuit of perfection will improve my life. Another piece of garbage that society peddles to you, which most of us consume during our upbringing. We are taught to respect perfection but never to examine this distorted notion. Because society glorifies this concept, which it regards as a symbol of self-worth and living a successful life, I refer to it as twisted. Unfortunately, there is no indication that people who strive for perfection are also successful in their pursuits. Instead, it opens a wide range of possibilities for clinical disorders.

Upgraditis

Perfectionism is a dangerous determination to achieve success at any cost. This chronic urge is developed out of a sense of regret when someone tells us that we are not good enough; the roots of this desire are firmly planted in self-hatred, and it brings up terrible memories of being rejected as children.

On the surface, society will respect perfectionists for their dedication, ambition, precision, and determination. However, the thought of impressing people by putting up extra effort captures their imaginations, such as when kids are praised for their academic achievements. Unfortunately, society frequently characterises them as individuals with high standards who put in twice as much effort as the next person; as a result, they frequently upset everyone with whom they live or work in their pursuit of perfection. My main issue is not with their performance, which is often good, but instead with their mental health.

A perfectionist family member makes life less enjoyable for everyone who lives under the same roof. Everyone despises a perfectionist at work for various reasons, including that they never fulfil deadlines and place greater emphasis on task perfection than on human interactions.

> *A team that includes more than one perfectionist will begin to show signs of decay while the project is still in progress; they will spend countless hours correcting something that doesn't need to be fixed.*

Perfectionists don't have many friends since they are constantly competing with others on standards in life, which makes them appear unfriendly. Perfectionists are characterised by their proclivity to under-budget their efforts to obtain a gold-plated outcome. Perfectionists cannot compute the difference between their grandiose vision and the average reality; as a result, they continue to push themselves and those involved in the process to attain their desired outcome. Even when the desired outcome is accomplished, they are dissatisfied because they believe something might have been done differently to give a better product. Their perfectionism serves as a cover for a variety of psychological issues.

The levels of perfection that are breeding in our society is unhealthy now. Perfection is rising to epidemic levels, especially among females. Society expects females to look a certain way. Just walk through the cosmetics sections of a departmental store; there is a product for every part of the body to make it look perfect. I was just curious, so I walked inside a famous department store to make a list of cosmetic categories sold to women for perfect looks; they are only hair and skins product categories. I found primers, concealers, foundations, blushers, bronzers, highlighters, eyeshadows, fake lashes, glitters, waterproofing products, eyeliners, mascaras, lipsticks, lip liners, lip pencils, tinting products, hair colours, face powders, nail polish, cleansers, face masks, toners, exfoliants, moisturisers, sunscreens, face creams, eye creams, neck creams, hand creams, creams for feet, night creams, day creams, acne creams, pigmentation creams, anti-age creams, body creams, face wash, body wash, vaginal wash, wet shampoos, dry shampoos, conditioners, skin toners, hair toners, essential oils, hair masks, gels, waxes, foams, mousses, serums, pomades, millions of perfumes, makeup brushes, eyeshadow brushes, sponges, curlers, dryers, straighteners, & hair sprays. All that is just for hair and skin only - let's not get started with other areas.

Despite this, women are under constant social pressure to be flawless. It is challenging to be a woman in western civilisation because society has certain expectations of women appearing in various situations. However, I am sure that there are fewer chemicals in my car's engine right now than there are on the skin and hair of some ladies.

Perhaps this imposed perfectionism interferes with women's ability to aggressively put themselves up for specific tasks in the corporate environment. For example, female candidates who have an 80 per cent skill match to a position description have, in my personal experience, been reluctant to apply for the position due to their belief that they will not be a perfect fit for the position. However, males who only has a 30 per cent skill match will be highly confident in their abilities. So, do you agree that society is subconsciously encouraging women to strive for perfection and that this expectation of perfection is causing women's lives to be harmed in the western world?

Young people nowadays have such false expectations of the perfect body, the perfect life, the perfect relationship, and the perfect social standing that they are influenced to achieve them with a vengeance.

Upgraditis

To spend more money on prestige objects and self-image, the younger generation is borrowing more money to look perfect. They also have unreasonable expectations of their life partners, thinking that they must be ideal in every way. We are evolving into a visual culture where appearance takes precedence over feelings. Society trains perfectionism to exist within a very narrow range of human possibilities. Society takes advantage of human vulnerabilities and uses them to create products and services to sell to them.

·······••••●•••••••···

The Mahabharata, one of the great Indian epics, contains an interesting plot. Draupadi was the name of a princess who lived in ancient India.

She was beautiful and talented; she accomplished something incredible, and one of the Gods was pleased with her dedication. As a result, God granted her one wish, which she knew precisely what she wanted. She wished for the ideal husband, the one who would be - the most righteous person on the face of the planet; also, the most powerful man on the planet; the best archer the world has ever seen; charming with a great sense of humour; and the most attractive man ever to have graced the face of the globe. She wished for a perfect husband who possessed all these characteristics, and

Upgraditis

God assured her that her wish for this perfect husband would be fulfilled at the right time.

Many years later, when the time came for her to get married due to unforeseen circumstances, she married five brothers known as the Pandavas, at the same time. Draupadi is one of the relatively few polyandrous women in Hindu mythology.

The five Pandava brothers were Yudhishthira, Bheema, Arjuna, Nakula, and Sahadeva. Yudhishthira was righteous; Bheema was the most powerful guy alive on the face of the globe; Arjuna was the best archer on the planet; Nakula was charming, and Sahadeva was the most attractive man on the planet.

Draupadi was enraged by the outcome and began blaming God. Finally, God appeared and stated that the characteristics you sought in a perfect husband were not present in any one man on this planet. So, the only way to fulfil your wish was to create circumstances where you get married to the five brothers simultaneously. So, I guess it was a win-win situation, given the impossible requirements for a perfect husband. I could just imagine how hard it would be to have five husbands.

Upgraditis

The moral of the story is that if you strive for perfection, you will be screwed multiple times.

·····•••••●•••••······

We have high achievers in our society, and often they are mistaken for perfectionists. Let us not confuse high achievers with perfectionists; there are differences.

Nothing less than perfection will suffice for perfectionists; anything less is a defeat. On the other hand, a high achiever can be content with doing a brilliant job and reaching excellence even if their grandiose ambitions aren't fully realised. Perfectionists are harsher on themselves and others than high achievers.

While high achievers are proud of their achievements and encourage others, perfectionists quickly point out flaws.

High achievers typically love the process of pursuing a goal just as much as or more than the destination itself. Perfectionists, on the other hand, see just the target. As a result, perfectionists often feel stiff when things don't go as planned.

Perfectionists are likewise far more terrified of failure than high achievers. Although it may seem incongruous that perfectionists are susceptible to procrastinating, which can be counterproductive, perfectionism and unproductivity tend to go hand in glove. It's because perfectionists, fearful of failure, can become frozen and fail to achieve anything at all if they worry too much about doing anything incorrectly. Procrastinating can increase emotions of inadequacy, reinforcing a vicious and paralysing cycle.

Since a less-than-perfect effort hurts and scares perfectionists, they react negatively to critical feedback. This distinguishes them from high performers who regard critique as valuable data for improving their future results. Perfectionists are frequently harsh on themselves, which can lead to low self-esteem. In the end, this can have a significant impact on a person's self-esteem and general happiness.

According to research, in today's western civilisation, one out of every three children will report clinically high levels of social perfection.

Please keep in mind that social perfection serves the demands of society rather than your own. As parents, we must encourage our children after they have tried and failed while refraining from acting like a helicopter parent, which might cause worry in our children.

Furthermore, we must establish a framework for determining when and where to prioritise competition and perfection.

No one is flawless. If we want to help our young people escape the trap of perfectionism, we will teach them that life will often defeat us in a chaotic world, but that's OK. Failure is not a weakness. If we want to help our young people outgrow this self-defeating snare of impossible perfection, then we will raise them in a society that has outgrown that very same delusion.

········●●●●●●●●●●●●●········

Once upon a time CEO of a construction goods company stated that he had separated the product development team into two groups. Specifically, "Team Quantity" will be rated purely on the "quantity" of work completed, while "Team Quality" will be graded solely on the "quality" of a single completed product.

During the final day of work, the CEO brings in his weighing scale to evaluate the performance of "Team Quantity." For example, if 500 Kg of clay was utilised to produce things, he would give it an "A," while 400 Kg would receive a "B." However, the team rated on "quality" just needed to produce one piece of product - and it had to be perfect - to receive an "A."

Upgraditis

When it came time to grade the work, a remarkable fact was discovered: all the highest quality pieces were produced by the group chasing quantity.

As a result, the "quantity" group was producing large quantities of work at a rapid pace while also learning from their failures. While the "quality" group sat about thinking about perfection, prominent people formed an innovation committee and steering committee to help them achieve their goals. They recruited a project manager to make things easy for the committee members. Unfortunately, the Project manager aggravated the issue by diverting the team's attention away from high-quality work and ineffective paper shuffling and reporting. The plan must then be developed, which requires meetings, status reports, a risk register, and a thousand and one other means by which productive activity was suppressed, and reality was filtered from reaching the decision-making committees, with little to show for their efforts other than grandiose theories on slides and a pile of dead clay.

Progress is hindered by the pursuit of perfection. Perfection is a symptom of a team's decline; perfection of planning is a cultural flaw of a team.

Upgraditis

So, if you write, code, design, or build things, start making stuff, which will lead to some good stuff. You can't make good stuff if you are not making a lot of stuff.

> *Perfectionism is a paranoid concept. However, a wise person recognises that life is an expedition, a never-ending journey of discovery by experimentation. That is the source of its excitement, the source of its energy.*

If you expect perfection from those around you, you will create challenges for yourself and others, and your existence will be nothing but suffering. As a result, a wise person accepts the imperfections of others while still appreciating them. If you love a woman, you should love her imperfections and shortcomings, just as she loves you with all your flaws and limitations. So don't be a perfectionist. If you happen to come across one, get away from them ASAP before they contaminate your thinking with their ideals.

Only insane people want perfection in all aspects of their lives. Perfectionism is an illness, and the more you want to be flawless, the more you'll become frustrated with your efforts to achieve perfection. As a result of humanity's relentless pursuit of perfection, we have come dangerously close to turning the globe into a mad asylum.

> *Perfection isn't something I advise; I don't preach perfection; instead, I preach the discipline of completeness. So instead of striving for perfection, try to complete things with discipline. Don't fall in love with perfection; instead, fall in love with a discipline of completeness of tasks.*

Don't try to perfect a recipe so you can impress your loved ones in a few weeks, instead try to cook for them every day, try to complete an imperfect recipe every day and eventually, excellence will emerge from your completeness.

Don't get frustrated if you don't have the perfect body shape; instead, try to complete 60 minutes of training every day, and in a few months, excellence will emerge from your discipline of completeness.

Don't look for perfect holidays in the perfect location once in 12 months; instead, try to take many small imperfect getaways throughout the year. The completion of those trips will bring more joy to your life than the perfect grandiose holidays.

Upgraditis

Don't try to finish a project with perfection, instead prioritise completeness, and if you have discipline, the result will be excellent, and you will have more time in your life to enjoy the outcome. Once you acknowledge what you have achieved, more positivity will enter your life. A person chasing perfection will never be happy with the outcome.

Strive for completeness of things as fast as possible instead of perfection. However, it is wise to pursue the discipline of completeness and achieve it than chase perfection forever. Would you choose a journey that will never end, or would you choose a destination that brings joy? I don't know about you, I chose the latter, which has brought me to a very peaceful place.

We must also learn how to separate the desire for perfection and the expectation of perfection. It is admirable and very human to strive for perfection, but it is equally human not to achieve it. There is no more growth or evolution if you are perfect. You're stuck if you're flawless. Perfection is synonymous with death; imperfection is synonymous with flow, growth, movement, and dynamism.

Upgraditis

The perfectionist has a goal in mind, whereas the person who loves to complete things has no sense of perfection; perfection only follows this person like a shadow from behind. Hence a person who chases completeness will be perfect, and this is the distinction between a perfectionist and a perfect person.

A perfectionist is chasing this shadow. It irritates this person as it is ahead of them. They are attempting to achieve it, sacrificing their present for the future, and if you get into the habit of sacrificing your present for the future, your entire life will be ruined.

So be a perfect person who likes to complete things and get things done as soon as possible. So, a perfect person will always be ahead of the perfectionist.

Upgraditis

I am not teaching you to be flawless; instead, I am teaching you to be complete. Be complete. Don't worry about being perfect. You will be flawed, but your flaws will be full of beauty, as they will be full of your completeness. If you try to be flawless, you will cause stress. There are already enough problems in your life; don't add to them.

I have experienced first-hand that perfection is one of the cornerstones of madness. We will never be 100% sane until we learn how to drop the concept of perfection. I am no longer a perfectionist now because circumstances have beaten this neuroticism out of me.

Upgraditis

My perspective changed; My flaws make me happy. Humanity appeals to me because it is flawed. It's flawed, which is why it's evolving; if it were flawless, it'd be extinct. Evolution is only conceivable in the presence of flaws. I want you to understand this: I am flawed, the entire universe is flawed, and my core message is flawed; this book is flawed, but I relish in this deficiency. I do not even expect you to be flawless. On the contrary, I want you to be as flawlessly flawed as possible. So, take pleasure in your flaws.

THE ADDICTION MYTH

Upgraditis

It appears like we are on a myth-busting rampage, as society's herd mentality has instilled so many lies in our collective consciousness. Another one of the myths I'd like to reveal is the addiction myth, which is a common misconception. Society told me that addiction was born from flawed character, which was a sign of lack of willpower. The society also told me that these addicts lack ethical principles. Society portrays addicts with some neurological disorder, and the medical community has been treating his disorder. The television portrayed them as desperate for some form of substance, but they don't say what's fuelling that desperation. As a result, you witness them acting in various dysfunctional ways, such as being aggressive, manipulative, or disagreeable. The media never explains why are they desperate. Society teaches us that addiction is an illness or a choice made by the individual, but this is entirely false. In reality, it is a human endeavour to temporarily escape from pain and misery. We overestimate the worth of nearby pleasures while underestimating the severity of their far-reaching repercussions, much like a youngster who believes his thumb is greater than the moon.

Have we been punishing people in our system who are trying to escape their pain and misery?

Upgraditis

There was one lady I worked with; she was hooked to poker. Once I witnessed her loose her monthly salary in a couple of hours in a famous casino in Melbourne. A few months later, I found out that her husband had left her due to the gambling addiction; I am sure she still thinks he is bluffing.

Middle-aged men are more prone to addictions because they are unsatisfied with their ordinary life and strive to be something greater than they are currently. There is no significance to their existence, and they seem to be dragging their lives along. Their lives are devoid of fragrance and colour; they live in an expansive desert that reaches as far as their eye can see, with no oasis in view. Occasionally, I wonder if mankind will ever be able to learn from its mistakes.

> *The same stupidity that God perpetrated*
> *with Adam and Eve continues today, namely,*
> *the imposition of bans. The fruit of this tree*
> *is not recommended for consumption. That,*
> *on the other hand, turns into an invitation.*

In a northwest state of India called Rajasthan, there has been growth in people getting addicted to snake bites. People who have been consuming certain drugs

Upgraditis

for a long time have now reached a point where these substances have no effect on their bodies, regardless of the amount. A cobra bite on their tongue is the only thing that provides them with some new experience. Anyone would die from that, but it is an excellent drug experience for them. It now getting evident that these guys have become addicted to cobra bites. Their entire bloodstream is poisoned. There have been instances when a cobra has died by biting these addicts on their tongues; the man has become highly poisonous, and the cobra is not poisonous over its entire body. Cobra has just a tiny gland that contains poison, and it is located in its mouth. According to the studies, the venom addicts reported euphoria, excessive pride, and extreme drowsiness for weeks. To get bitten on the tip of the tongue, they enlisted the services of snake charmers. They reported feeling higher stimulation and a sensation of well-being after the bite, which they said was more potent than a normal concentration of alcohol or opioid. So how do people who use opioids deal with poisonous snake bites? The doctors speculate that snake venom neurotoxins bind to nicotinic acetylcholine receptors. These receptors play a role in euphoria, sadness, and depression, explaining the high.

Upgraditis

Let's get this straight: addiction is when you do the same thing over and over again. If you do the same thing over and over again, you're going around in circles. Being a slave to repetitiveness is a terrible crime against one's own life. The mind likes to work in repetition, as it prefers to work from its memories. However, because the mind is always thinking about the past, it repeatedly tends to do the same things.

I don't know any cocaine addicts that I am aware of. But I have known people with addictions my entire life. When I was growing up, my relative was addicted to alcohol; over the number of years, I witnessed this man with unlimited potential, family, employment and an excellent home lose everything to his addiction with the bottle. Alcohol ruined him financially morally, made him dishonest, destroyed his reputation, lost his self-respect, broke the hearts of his loved ones, and almost killed him. I saw a man tied with a chain to the bottle until he destroyed everything in his life.

When I moved to Australia in my early 20's, I quickly realised that the western world was struggling with addiction more than the less technologically advanced east. I had front row seats to a culture that was vulnerable to all sorts of crazy habits. I witnessed young men and women not getting enough sleep because they were addicted to something. I witnessed a new phenomenon that I only saw in movies with white people on TV. I got introduced to the concept of nightlife. In India, where I grew up, energy generation was a problem, so it became expensive to fund entertainment at scale once the sun went down. But things were different in Australia; everything lights up at night - the clubs, bridges, roads, the billboards, the massive Coca-Cola sign at Kings cross, the skyline. It was a party town. Now I lived in a rich country where energy was produced to support a nightlife lifestyle utterly unnatural for humans. For hundreds and thousands of years, nighttime was when we were scared and slept in the cave or on the trees. This electricity has changed our games; we started becoming nocturnal animals.

My Eastern philosophy taught me that only three kinds of people are awake at night. The Rogi, Bhogi & Yogi.

Rogi means someone suffering from a physical or mental illness. Someone who can't sleep because of physical or psychological pain.

Upgraditis

Bhogi means an addict—addicted to a substance, pleasure-seeking or screens.

Yogi means someone who religiously practises yoga or meditation. Some Yogi's put them in a state where they were unaware of the time of day and would meditate for days.

I doubt that people queuing outside the nightclubs at 2 am are Yogi's. All the people I saw getting excited and running around late at night were either Rogi's or Bhogi's. These Rogi's and Bhogi's struggled to wake up every morning and created long queues outside the coffee shops, an addictive chemical widely sold in the western world that gives you energy, focus but the trade-off was more anxiety. I saw the majority of the people I worked with could not function without this chemical - they were hooked. They were chained to the cup. Western society forgets that proper focus happens when you are alert and calm. When you are alert and anxious - you are jittery.

People enslaved by the cup were queuing outside bars after work for a glass of wine or a pint of beer. The Rogi's and Bhogi's of the society didn't like freedom. When one chain came off, they demanded and craved another chain. The big corporations were capitalising on Rogi's and Bhogi's; they were building more and more products for these addicts. These junkies had forgotten the pleasures of ordinary living. Addiction to the cup, addiction to the bottle, addiction to nicotine or smoking, addiction to a psychoactive substance, addiction to the phone, addiction to spending/shopping, addiction for social validation, addiction to virtual relationships, and so on are some of the most common addictions in the Western world.

> *All addictions fall into one of three groups.*
> *First is an addiction to sensation. Second, there*
> *is an addiction to security, with the pursuit of*
> *security being the leading cause of insecurity.*
> *The third is an addiction to power and control.*

Addicts frequently link a feeling of exhilaration with their initial encounter with the addictive substance. But, on the other hand, the human body makes it physically impossible to recreate that original sensation. The result is frequently a gradual loss of any feeling, which eventually becomes utterly devastating in all facets of the addict's life.

I worked with a colleague who would run to the pub mid-day because the stress of project delivery was getting to them, and the only way to feel better was to have a couple of drinks. I worked with another gentleman who would borrow money from coworkers and go to the pub for a drink since his wife had taken control of the funds. These men work in high profile jobs, have been to excellent schools and have a lot of talent. But, they are like that elephant, that has forgotten that he is an elephant, chained to a bottle - unable to move, and every day they get weaker and weaker.

Now things are getting worse; little kids getting addicted to video games. In the 1950s, an average 10-year old kid in western society would usually drift away in a radius of 8 km away from their homes with their friends or alone to play or explore. In the 1980s, that radius of exploration shrank to 5km and had been shrinking ever since. I have experienced now that ten-year-old kids would never leave alone to go anywhere. Their autonomy radius is probably less than one kilometer. I know families that never let their 10-year-old kids leave home alone, ever. On the contrary, society has become safer in the last 70 years.

A famous professor of psychology in Vancouver carried out a sadistic experiment earlier in the 20th century. It involves a rat, yes the creature, if killed in large amounts in a scientific laboratory, can get you a

UPGRADITIS

PhD degree. Professor got a healthy rat, put it in a cage, and was given two water bottles. One was just water, and the other was water mixed with cocaine. So now this rat is frantically hunting for a way out of the cage; all of this rushing about has made this rat thirsty. So rat tries out water from both bottles. Unfortunately, he gets hooked to the cocaine water as he gets a kick out of it; this rat now never goes to the plain water bottle. The Cocaine water would put this rat in a euphoric state. The rat would have lots of energy will be mentally alert for a very long time. Now this rat started trying out crazy shit to get out of the cage. Once the rat noticed a performance drop, he would run toward the water bottle with cocaine to get recharged. After a few days, the honeymoon period of cocaine was over; now rat was experiencing tremors, muscle cramps, restlessness, irritability, panic, anxiety and paranoia. In addition, the professor noticed that rats body temperature went up with the heart rate and blood pressure. The rat also developed disruption in heart rhythm constricted blood vessels with neurological disorders. Now, this poor rat was addicted to cocaine; he started consuming more than average water every day as the reward circuitry in the brain began to get numb. The rat would need more and more amounts of cocaine every day to feel energetic. Cocaine has now completely changed the brain wiring of this poor creature; this little rats behaviour is now erratic, violent and downright bizarre. One day professor returned to the lab and noticed that this rat had killed himself with a cocaine overdose. So the experiment was repeated again, resulting in the same outcome. After that, the professor became famous for his work with addiction.

Another professor came along a few decades later and looked at the experiment once more. This professor was a creative thinker who wanted to re-create the experiment with tweaks. First and foremost, he opted not to use the cage. Instead, he plans to construct a Disney-themed rat park. The Disney park for rats is fantastic; it has an entertainment section, a rat gym, a few coloured bells and many cheese balls spinning around, a network of tunnels to explore, and many other props to make this an adventure. For a rat, being here was a dream come true. Secondly, the professor smarty pants brought many rat relatives, rat friends, and rat kids to the rat park. It was the most fantastic rat community on the face of the earth. Thirdly, professor smarty pants never changed the water bottles, one of which was filled with regular water and the other with cocaine. The astounding discovery was that the rats rarely drank from the drugged bottle, consuming normal water instead. As a result, none of them became addicted to the toxic water, and none of the rats overdosed. Going from a 100 per cent overdose to a 0 per cent overdose was fascinating. This was done repeatedly, with the same result each time.

Professor smarty pants worked it out; the problem was not the addiction but the cage. The community rats were living a happy, connected and active life. So do you now understand how addiction works?

I have seen so many people addicted to a substance and spending most of their useful lives in a cage. Unfortunately, the medical system has been treating them in the cage. You would argue that this doesn't work with Humans as we are much more intelligent than rats, and our needs are entirely different. However, history has witnessed this cage experiment with Humans. In the '70s, American troops were fighting a war with the Vietnamese gorilla forces. America started losing as the shit hit the fan, the American soldiers started breaking. A quarter of American troops in Vietnam got addicted to heroin. It was their escape from reality - it was challenging and broke them mentally and physically. The American news publications were paranoid about what would happen if these soldiers who had become addicts would come back home. They were reporting that there will be hundreds and thousands of Heroin addicts on the street of the USA when the war finishes.

War finished, America lost. Soldiers came home, and the American Society of Psychiatry was expecting that the rehabs would be complete and many soldiers would go into withdrawal. So what happened was that 95% of the soldiers just stopped using heroin once they were reunited with their families, kids, friends, hobbies and freedom. The cage was not there, so there was no desire to return to the substance.

So professor smarty pant was right; it's not about chemicals. It's about the cage.

> *Maybe addiction is the adaption to your hostile environment. Perhaps the substance addiction is a bond to the hostile environment you live in. Human beings are an emotional soup of flesh and blood, we have a natural and inherent need to form a bond, and when we're happy and healthy, we'll bond and connect.*

Still, if you can't do that because you're traumatised or isolated or beaten down by life, we tend to bond with something that will give us temporary relief. It could be gambling, pornography, cocaine, cannabis, but you will bond and connect with something because that's our nature. So almost everything we think we know about addiction is wrong. These addictions happened in the lives of people who lacked meaningful bonds and meaningful relationships. So they felt trapped in the cage just like that rat. The only way was to sip on the drugged water as it brought some excitement, momentarily. But it was killing them.

Few of my friends and even family members went through massive surgeries. After the surgery, they were given a diamorphine drip controlled by the patient. Diamorphine is pure medical-grade heroin. Can you imagine how many people in the world go for surgeries every day and then gets exposed to heroin every day? They are exposed to chemical hooks. Do they become addicts? They don't get addicted because they have connections and bonds in their life. They have people to love.

There are various reasons why society's need for alcohol is increasing. One thing is sure; individuals are not constantly battling for their survival. A sizeable portion of the population has shifted out of survival mode. People must find other focus points and passionate commitment once they have progressed beyond survival. If this does not occur, the need for enjoyment and alcohol will inevitably increase in that society. This is why, even if parents are wealthy, their children must not experience wealth until they reach a particular age. Another factor is that both parents work in most cases these days. As a result, the youngster does not receive the attention that they require at a young age.

Furthermore, there is insufficient regular exercise. When you don't enjoy your body's natural health and the vibrancy and vigour of your mechanism, alcohol is the only thing you'll enjoy. Drugs are being used for more than just euphoria; they also make people feel alive for a few hours. As a result, the generation as a whole is moving in that direction. It is critical to engage them in sports and other vigorous activities that connect them to nature, such as hiking, rock climbing, diving, and so on. In addition, they must develop a passion for something, such as painting or music.

Why does society mistake addiction as a character flaw? First, society sees addiction as a moral failing. So what do we do with people with addictions - We

UPGRADITIS

punish them, stigmatise them, shame them and create special facilities where we isolate them and break all their connections. We make them social outcasts and also give them criminal records. We put barriers between them reconnecting. The systems we have built do the exact opposite to break addiction patterns. The number of natural, meaningful friendships one person has been declining steadily. The amount of space an individual has in their home has been steadily growing, we've traded floorspace for buddies, and we've traded boxes for connections.

Connection is the solution for all addictions; if you are addicted to caffeine or alcohol, you have lost the connection with your inner self to generate a state of joy or alertness. If you are addicted to shopping, you need to connect with people who don't have much in life. If you are addicted to porn, you are not connected to someone who can fill the empty space between your fingers. If you are addicted to video games and screens, you are not connected to sunshine. If you are addicted to liquor, you are not connected to your body's chemicals while exercising and sweating. Something is wrong with us; we've created a society where many of us, life looks like a cage and a whole lot less like rat Disney Park. Instead, look for relationships and bonds with people and purpose; these connections will bring joy to your life. You are not addicted. You lack connections.

Your Superpowers

UPGRADITIS

Several misconceptions about mental wellbeing exist in our society, such as that mental illnesses signify weakness; contrary to this belief, however, the opposite is true. Trying to fight a mental health disorder requires a massive amount of strength. Historically mental disorders were often portrayed as manifestations of poor character or a lack of self-discipline while media demonised mental illnesses. Yet another myth that I've heard is that people who suffer from mental illnesses are usually aggressive and erratic. This is also entirely wrong; in fact, those who suffer from mental illness are at a higher of risk victimisation and unexpected reaction from others. Also, I'd like to emphasise that mental health issues have nothing to do with being a slacker or a weakling. In the U. S., suicide is the tenth most common cause of death; it is responsible for more than 41,000 deaths each year, well over twice the number of murders.

My beloved grandmother, with whom I shared a home, was afflicted with severe depression almost her entire life. While growing up, I witnessed her suffering the hardships provoked by this dark cloud. It is difficult for young children to watch their loved ones suffer as kids don't know how to help. However, I could never relate to her suffering since I was too young to grasp the complexities of the human brain, and I didn't know enough about mental illnesses. Her seasonal depression began in the first week of autumn and lasted through the winter months; she rarely left her room during this period. Because of the sedative medications prescribed by the psychologist, none of the family's kids could spend much time with her while she was down. My grandmother's demeanour would change dramatically as the days became longer and the spring season approached. We could see her transform into a hypomanic state where she was full of energy and became immensely social during the summer months. Unfortunately, she suffered from this vicious cycle of seasonal illness all her life; her major depressive state would return when the autumn season commenced.

I spoke to her for the last time during the second week of autumn in 2004, just as she was beginning to have seasonal depression symptoms. Unfortunately, after tolerating this emotional pain for decades, she passed away from a cardiovascular condition. She was a wonderful soul. When she was at her best in the summer months, she would act like social glue and an entertainer. The fact that I was unable to assist her in overcoming her mental condition was one of the greatest regrets of my life. I was always a spectator to her emotional pain as a kid.

As I grew older, I began researching mental illnesses and started to work with people who were depressed and anxious. Trust me, they are not hard to find. So I started to assist people with symptoms of depression, overcoming negative and self-limiting notions to regain their vitality, optimism and zest for life's pleasures. It made me feel good to bring a smile to the face of someone suffering from depression, and it helped me make peace with my past.

I'm not here to provide you with a cure for your mental disorder. I'm sorry, but I don't have any prescriptions that make you feel better. So instead, the purpose of this chapter is to provide you with a distinctive perspective on mental disorders. My goal is to alter your perceptions of mental illness and tell you more about these desirable disadvantages.

So what is a desirable disadvantage?

> *Individuals with more prominent eyeballs have gorgeous eyes, but their eyes sights are not the best as they grow older. So this is called a desirable disadvantage.*

Upgraditis

Another example would be being born in a very wealthy household, which is desirable. The data is apparent that kids born in very wealthy households lack fulfilment, ambition, a sense of self-worth, and they spend 40% of their lives in a depressive state. So this is a desirable disadvantage. Finally, consider the case of dyslexia; businessmen Richard Branson, who has dyslexia. Instead of dwelling on his limitations, he devised workarounds. He honed his problem-solving skills to an art form. Almost all dyslexics have this ability - but society makes them believe that something is terribly wrong with them.

Before we dive deep into extracting advantages from mental illness, let us first understand the anthropology of mental conditions.

The majority of cavemen and women, according to anthropologists, were suffering from Bipolar Disorder out of necessity a few hundred thousand years ago. Their lifestyles were controlled by seasons, so when springtime arrived, and summertime started to take hold, they would surface and gather and hunt enough food to last them for a few months. As a result, they would go into a hypomanic state. They became superhuman hunters and gatherers, and they were also highly sexual since they needed to have many children to sustain the group's population at a healthy level. So they would hunt and collect all summer long, and then as the days grew smaller and the evening grew slightly cooler, they would begin to slip into the period of depression, where they would become less interested in sex, and they would find a place to take cover and stay warm, keeping the children alive until the summertime. When I looked into the behaviour patterns of our forefathers, I was able to make a direct connection between them and the depressive and hypomanic phases that my grandmother went through. This is not anecdotal; instead, it is a well-documented fact that the consumption of antidepressants increases during the winter months. In most cases, this is due to a lack of sunlight, which affects serotonin levels and mood patterns.

> *I wonder whether depression is nature's norm*
> *of keeping us safe. We must then ask if*
> *other mental disorders from that era were just*
> *mother natures survival skills?*

Therefore, why did Mother Nature leave such genes in our bodies if depression wasn't a survival skill?

Upgraditis

The majority of art is the consequence of depression, and multiple studies have shown that artists are significantly more likely than those in other occupations to be depressed. In my experience, psychiatrists label such creative types as "depressed" because they prefer to spend their time alone creating art or conversing with their inner monologue. Of course, I'm not suggesting that you should get depressed at this time, but I'm attempting to highlight the impact on the creative business as a whole. They can transform a depressing vision into magnificent art. But, on the other hand, art cannot exist in its original form if depression doesn't really exist.

Children are labelled with attention deficit disorder and attention deficit hyperactivity disorder in today's schools. The use of ADHD medications by children is approaching epidemic proportions. For low-level, tedious clerical labour at schools, teachers request parents take their children to the doctor and medicate them. Nowadays, we make fun of children for disrupting class because they are chained to a desk for six and a half hours and forced to look at a whiteboard. However, it was not amusing when we were hunter-gathers when anything and everyone might kill you. ADHD was a life-saving skill. According

Upgraditis

to a study conducted in Kenyan nomadic tribes, those with greater levels of ADHD lived in a more confident and well-nourished group. When we lived as hunter-gatherers, we would have perished if not for the ADHD adults who defended our communities. As a result of this genetic variation, we have this ability, now categorised as an illness. It's difficult for students with this gene variant to concentrate on a single task at a time in the classroom. Still, this mutation in our forefathers shielded them from livestock raids, muggings, and dangers from predatory animals.

Gillian Lynne was diagnosed with a learning disorder by her schoolteacher, and she was referred to a doctor for further evaluation. ADHD has not yet been given a name. Wriggle Bottom was the name of the disorder. So her mother took Gillian to see a doctor, who turned on the radio after hearing everything about her daughter's hyperactivity from her mother. Gillian began bouncing, twirling, and dancing as if nothing had happened. Finally, the doctor advised that you take your daughter to a dance school because she is talented. The mother acknowledged the wise words from the doctor and did so. Today, Jillian is a filthy rich woman responsible for some of the most important theatre productions of our time, such as Phantom of the Opera and Cats. Consider that if Gillian's mum took her to the psychologist or psychiatrist today, he would have given her amphetamines, and she would have become an accountant because society judges a fish on its ability to climb up a tree.

Another mental illness that receives excellent attention is obsessive-compulsive disorder. When we were hunter-gatherers, we had to stockpile months of food supply to last through the winter months. So choosing a quartermaster or supply sergeant preoccupied with cleanliness and organisation would be a great idea. But, unfortunately, that's someone who suffers from obsessive-compulsive disorder. Back then, it was a necessary trait for surviving.

Dyslexics have a unique ability to see the world around them. When most people look, they see what is directly in front of them. However, dyslexics have an incredible knack for identifying the abnormality due to their sharper peripheral vision.

Other capabilities, such as enhanced listening and vibrational sensitivity, can be used to compensate for the lack of vision in a blind person's mind. Blind superhero Daredevil has enhanced residual senses and uses them to his advantage. Evidence implies that learned behaviour improves remaining senses: blind persons pay more attention to other cues and are programmed to use them more effectively without sight. It is the brain's way of making up for the damage. Brain areas previously used to process sensory information are rewired to deal with other activities or sensations lost by a skill. A deaf person's brain undergoes remarkable rewiring, which we've seen firsthand. The brain region that processes sound has been reassigned to handle something else, such as touch or vision. Because of this plasticity, certain aspects of our brains are susceptible to change. It has been demonstrated that neuroplasticity is both a cause and a remedy for mental illness.

Upgraditis

As a result, I adhere to the fundamental tenet that where you look determines where you drive. Focusing on abilities makes you stronger. You get weaker if you focus on the suffering. Blindness and mental depression are examples of the brain's inability to perceive light. Depression starts to fade away as soon as the process of developing one's future gets underway. Depression could be our brain's inability to construct a future.

In addition to the emotional agony of mental disorders, some abilities are also acquired. You may have superpowers that your psychologist and physiatrist haven't told you about. It would be beneficial to learn to use your powers instead of focusing on your emotional misery. Avoid being among people who will bring you closer to your emotional suffering. Someone who can't handle the worst of you doesn't deserve the best of you. Let's talk about some powers that certain mental conditions bring along.

Anxiety is a state of fear, worry and uneasiness. An anxious mind will wander through the endless adverse outcomes for a possible terrifying future.

They are like smoke alarms for any possible danger. It is like a conspiracy theorist living in your head who doesn't shut up and forces you to listen to all the scary outcomes. Anxiety is our brains upgrade mechanism to increase the IQ, as it causes the neurons to make new connections. It studied a direct correlation between anxiety with the Jewish community and their high IQ. In addition, individuals with a generalised anxiety disorder are also linked to high verbal skills and high levels of empathy for others. Empathy is heightened emotional intelligence and speaking skills. So, it is a great superpower to have in specific fields like customer services, health care etc.

Someone suffering from Bipolar will experience sates of depression followed by mania and a feeling of grandiosity. The depression phase gives them heightened empathy and resilience in life. It has also been noted that bipolar people have a fantastic sense of smell. In the Manic phase, they will act on their grandiose theories and have the energy to bring them to life. A manic person will have the energy and ideas to build things that have never been made.

The famous maths genius, John Nash, suffered from Schizophrenia. Many studies have indicated that

Upgraditis

Maths geniuses suffer from psychosis. He was made famous by the film A beautiful mind. Schizophrenia alters one's perception of reality in more favourable ways to deduce mathematical equations.

People suffering from the obsessive-compulsive disorder have memory hoarding problems; they have developed fantastic memory due to his practice. All studies on obsessive-compulsive disorder patients indicate that these individuals have unforgettable memory as their brain area responsible for retraining information is enlarged compared to the rest of the population.

We relate Tourettes to someone shouting out obscenities and having no control over them. A mind of a person with Tourettes is in a constant battle with controlling unwanted impulses. This uncomfortable process gives these individuals extra cognation to control what they can manage. These individuals do very well in sports, where control is required - This could explain the secret behind the ball precision of David Beckham or the NBA superstar, Chris Jackson. Anthony Ervin attributes his swimming skills to Tourette's, making his reflexes faster. I remember going to school with a twitchy friend; he was average in everything in life, but he could bowl Yorkers after

Yorkers in cricket; I don't know where he is. Maybe society pushed him to become an average software developer somewhere.

A person with ADHD gets more ideas before 9 am than any other person throughout the day. ADHD allows them to take more risks, resulting in more creative thinking. An ADHD brain has no tolerance for tedious, repetitive work; that is their reason for the restlessness. Their brains focus on things of interest, especially with risk-taking jobs. Creativity is a risk we take every day in our careers, hobbies and cooking. Creative minds are risk-takers as they challenge beliefs and everyday thinking. Their minds are impulsive, so they are quick decision makers - it is a great survival skill to have. The ADHD mind will instantly switch off the stupid risk analysis matrix and find a creative solution. ADHD brain likes daydreaming, as they are developing innovative adaptions to different situations that may happen. Now tell me what Will Smith, Justin Timberlake and Michael Phelps have in common. Yep, you guessed it right.

Two of the most intelligent personalities born on the planet have been Autistic, i.e. Newton & Einstein. The data shows that around 15% of people on the

Autism spectrum are Savants; they are the best in one area of their interest. It could be mathematics, art, Music, Science or stacking shelves at the supermarket. One of the local supermarkets in Sydney used Autistic teenagers to stack products on shelves, and it was a mind-blowing shopping experience. A paradise for OCD people. Their superpower is their memory, hyper focus and ability to retrieve information for the area of interest.

Look around; the people who built this entire world around us are the ones that clinicians would call mentally ill. So let's talk about some geniuses, and I will also list their mental illness next to them.

Issac Newton - Bipolar, Autism, Schizophrenia

Albert Einstein - Autism

Elon Musk - Aspergers Syndrome

Leo Tolstoy - Depression

Winston Churchill - Bipolar disorder

Charles Darwin - Agoraphobia

Michelangelo - Autism

Ab Lincoln - Depression

Steve Jobs - obsessive-compulsive disorder

Upgraditis

Beethoven - Bipolar disorder

Van Gogh - Bipolar disorder

Nikola Tesla - Obsessive-compulsive disorder

Kanye west - Bipolar disorder

> *When you think about it, most superheroes have some form of issue or tragedy in their lives. Superman was launched into space in a capsule, and his planet exploded. If you take him to a psychologist, he will be diagnosed with separation anxiety and will be on a pill.*

When Batman was a kid, he witnessed his parents being shot on the street. According to the doctor, there is post-traumatic stress disorder (PTSD). Hulk obviously has intermittent explosive disorder, but he has learnt to use it to his advantage.

So, how did this society condition you? And you never look at the benefits that these mental conditions bring. While people suffering from mental health issues are confused about their reality, society capitalised on the opportunity to build new products, services and professions. Society reinforced their belief that something was wrong with them through those products, services, and professions. I experienced that society was putting the chains around the necks of people who experienced mental health issues; most of the time, the chain was tethered to a pill. So, who is the domesticated elephant now?

People, groups, and cultures who emphasise their strengths are more likely to succeed than those that emphasise their weaknesses. Recognise and capitalise on your own abilities. Rather than comparing oneself to others, look for people who motivate or encourage you for your own growth. Use the strengths of others to offset your own weaknesses. Although no one could be a master at everything, most of us are fortunate enough to be encircled by others who are.

The human body is a very complex chemical factory. We are depriving the mind and body of nature and natural things that have been bringing joy to us for millions of years. In addition, we are creating certain pharmacological deficiencies in our bodies. As a result, we don't feel good, and now we need a Psychologist or a Psychiatrist. Psychology and Psychiatry are the only medical science branches where the doctor doesn't examine the organ or body to diagnose problems. Instead, they will ask you some questions and collect data. Then this data is plotted against the rest of humanity to see where you sit. If what you experience is way above the median population, it's classified as mental illness; then they have a pill for you. Alternatively, if what you experience is way below what the median population feels, you have a mental health condition, and they have another pill for you. Their principle is that if you are not like the majority, something is wrong. Psychology is not an exact science because psychology doesn't meet the five basic requirements for any stream to be considered scientifically correct. Those requirements are Clearly defined terms, Quantifiability, Controlled & accurate experiments, Reproducibility & Ability to predict & test. Psychology fails the first two requirements for it to be called a science.

So what if those of us diagnosed with mental illness have remarkable evolutionary adaptation? And if that is the case, why do we call it mental illness, not mental able-ness? What would the impact be on a child if you could convince them that what they have is not simply a mental illness but mental able-ness? So I believe the positive impact would be incalculable. Pain has a

UPGRADITIS

bond with life, and it will be always there. So, instead, work on your strengths; with new powers comes new responsibility. Do you want to sit still chained to the pill? or do you enjoy shattering the chains and figuring out new ways to create leverage with your newly discovered superpowers.

THE WEB OF BELIEFS

UPGRADITIS

I have studied belief systems for the last two decades. However, my journey with belief started in childhood, like most of us. I studied almost all the major religions and belief systems in my pursuit to understand the world. While researching belief systems, I started noticing that five things were shared by all human civilisations around the planet. They are linguistics, toolmaking, music or singing, artwork, and beliefs. Apart from beliefs, all other elements have their origins in the animal world.

Any belief system has a simple thought architecture, punishes knowledge, inquiry, and rewards obedience and compliance.

Beliefs are a human-centric phenomenon as we have developed a frontal lobe in our brain that enables us to imagine. No other species can imagine; try explaining the meaning of tomorrow to your dog.

In addition, I travelled to remote places and explored the belief systems of indigenous tribes. Once I got introduced to a flat earth believer, I absolutely loved my time with him - It was really entertaining for me.

UPGRADITIS

Some of my friends believe that we never landed on the moon. I find it amusing; it makes me think about why people believe what they believe.

People believe in religions, gods, holy books, UFO's, aliens, haunted houses, monsters, devils, deities, angels, hell, heaven, big-foot, cults and conspiracy theories. On the other hand, some believe that God does not exist. It's not uncommon for people to believe in tooth fairies, Santa Claus, and even the afterlife. I also have friends who believe we are in a simulation and our universe exists inside a computer program controlled by an alien race. Almost everyone lives in a free country, so they can believe in anything they like.

> *All humans are born with zero belief systems; it is not natural to humans.*

However, we are born with the intelligence and curiosity to understand phenomena around us. Kids are full of curiosity, and they are constantly experimenting with things around them to understand them better. People around us do not like to say, "I do not know, " which is why we start teaching kids our belief systems; it is a lack of understanding. Although "I do not know" has a minimal shelf life, people will eventually start looking for the truth; because nobody can live with "I do not know" for long. Why don't people believe in trees, sun, sky, water or gravity? It may be because they exist. However, people believe in Gods, heaven, hell, astrology and the afterlife; these are beliefs because we do not know.

> *Belief is a substitution for understanding;*
> *it is deceptive. The institutions built by*
> *belief are incentivised to keep people in a*
> *state of ignorance.*

Once people have drowned in their ignorance of 'I do not know', their belief will grow with time. Once they have believed in something for a very long time, they will be fooled by their mindset so profoundly that they will not suspect it. This will slowly transform into delusion, which will eventually become defective wisdom. Once this starts happening, they will be mentally vulnerable, and they can be made to do anything based on this defective wisdom.

All major belief systems have been around for a long time; they were built by people who promote ignorance in society. In this case, ignorance leads to darkness, and this is how people were manipulated, subjugated, trapped in poverty by the authorities. Society has taught you to believe more and more. All the belief you have in your life is just a cover for your insecurities. The more insecure you are, the more you will believe in things.

The masses regard belief as accurate, the wise as false, and leaders as useful. Belief systems employ various methods to keep their supporters together and prohibit mixing. I also noticed that having a belief provides consolation in difficult times. Believers can also comfort themselves by remembering that the invisible man in the sky has a reason for their suffering. Belief also gives them the certainty that things will be far better in the next life, even if things are difficult now. The evolutionary benefit of combining hostility and beliefs to discriminate against others is quite common. Humans evolved over millions of years in an environment where there was only enough food for one's own group. Any other group they encountered represented a fatal threat and had to be killed. Aggression and tribalism are evolutionary features of our belief systems that cannot be eradicated by a generation of Uber eats and aisles filled with breakfast cereals. This also helps us to explain why xenophobia persists in our society.

Upgraditis

The level of religious belief in society is affected by economic status. For example, people in developed countries don't believe in God as much as people in poorer countries. Japan, for instance, has one of the best living standards and practices, but only 50% of its people say they're religious. In Western Europe and Australia, there has been a similar pattern: more and more people are giving up their religious views. On the other hand, compared to the rest of the developed world, the USA has a high standard of living, and a considerable amount of people have religious beliefs. However, compared to Japan, Western Europe, and Australia, the USA does not have universal health care and extensive social safety nets. So, the government will not help you as much as other places in the developed world. American society makes people's futures less secure, which makes the idea of a good heavenly father more enticing.

As more and more people in the western world are dropping religious beliefs, they are also picking up new ones. When people process information that backs up their beliefs, they get a dopamine rush, making them feel happy.

Upgraditis

All belief systems you have right now are limiting your growth, even the positive self-belief models you get from the motivational gurus online.

> *People who get accustomed to believing will keep looking for more things of similar nature; they get addicted to this mental state of servitude, as seeking the truth is hard.*

Belief doesn't solve any of humanity's problems now; it has a net-zero impact on our planet and wastes everyone's time.

·····•••••●•••••••···

Two wise men once resided in a village in India. The first was a religious man, whereas the second was an atheist. Their religious views were on the far side of the spectrum. Because of these two well-educated locals, the entire community was confused. The theist used the scriptures to explain the existence of God to the locals. On the other hand, the atheist used his cleverness to dismiss all theists' assertions. People in the village were split; they didn't know who to follow and avoid.

One of the village elders recommended that these two should debate in front of the entire community.

Upgraditis

As a result, the entire community will unanimously follow the belief system of the winner.

The debate started one fine morning, and the entire village gathered to watch. First, the atheist was disproved by the theist's presentation of his religious views. The atheist then argued against theism and gave all his evidence for atheism. The debate lasted 24 hours, and by the following day, something interesting happened; the theist had converted into an atheist, and the atheist had converted into a theist. Both of them were persuaded by each other's world-views.

In the end, the issue was not settled. However, because the two men had persuaded and agreed with each other, the village still had an atheist and a theist; thus, the aggregate remained constant, and the villager's predicament remained intact.

Moral of the story: Believing or disbelieving something will just waste your time and will not move you any closer to the truth.

······••••●•••••••···

You can travel to China and Saudi Arabia and observe the polar opposite belief systems; one disbelieves in all kinds of believing, and the other beliefs in just one kind of believing. On the surface, they look different, but once you get a bit deeper, you will observe that disbelief is as ignorant as belief. Both accept things without inquiry. Both trust and have faith in an ideology, but they don't verify.

Superstitious belief systems were standard in hunter-gatherer societies, but no organised religion existed back then. Humans began to adopt agriculture about 10,000 years ago. The world eventually shifted solely to farming and herding. Compared to hunting and gathering, agriculture can support many more people per acre of land, but at a cost. Every day, you spend time with the same group of 100 people or so. You get to know them very well this way. As long as we kept our group sizes small, we had the reasoning to deal with community members effectively. As the population started getting more prominent due to the food surpluses, we eventually started building villages, towns, and cities. Now, the vast majority of people you engaged with regularly were complete strangers to you. At this point in time, we were experiencing a shift in cultural values. Human survival was now dependent on the ability to work together.

Individuals who cheated or committed an immoral act were quickly disciplined by their peers in small groups. But, this was not the case when we started living in large groups; it became easier to take advantage of others in large anonymous neighbourhoods. So, the solution was to create gods who were constantly on the lookout for cheaters and who would punish them in the afterlife. The growth of all major religions overlaps with the development of urban areas worldwide. So that's how Jesus became an unpaid babysitter for all the kids. There was a widespread belief in one or more gods who watch our actions and judge us due to our actions. Gods were also created to explain the gaps in human knowledge; we didn't understand the thunder, so it must be Thor. Now the society feeds you bullshit by mentioning that God has a plan for you, seriously?

> *All beliefs provide a false security blanket, like praying to solve real-world situations. When a person starts making invisible friends, we start treating them for Schizophrenia, but when a group of people make an invisible friend and start talking to them daily, we consider it normal because it's called praying.*

Upgraditis

Unfortunately, sometimes kids get indoctrinated with the concept of praying to solve real-life problems. As a result, they usually grow up as irresponsible adults who cannot solve any problems.

For example, you give a man fish, you feed him for a day. Teach him how to fish, and you provide him for life. Now, you give this man a belief system, and he will pray for fish all his life. Belief indicates your ignorance and gives you false hopes.

In India, there is a significant dependence on Jyotish - The ancient Hindu astrology. Astrologers are consulted for everything, even when starting any new venture. They claim to solve all your financial, professional or personal problems; they will prescribe you specific gemstones to fix the fault in your stars. Usually, fear is used to make people believe in the solutions they offer. The number of gemstones an Indian man/woman wears is directly proportional to their insecurities. The more beliefs you will have, the more insecure you will be, the less you will inquire, and the less you will seek or explore. A person of belief will be stuck in that mental prison, and no amount of evidence provided will free them from that prison.

Things quickly escalate when two or more belief systems clash.

> *All the global conflict comes from one group's beliefs versus other groups beliefs.*

This conflict is happening because these groups believe. People who flew planes into those buildings believed they were doing the right thing. Some people blow themselves to pieces and kill innocent kids, men and women - because they believe they will be in a beautiful place after that.

> *Beliefs entrap our minds like a prisoner. One thing seems sure: humanity will continue to be dominated if they believe what they are fed. As long as individuals are directed to believe, they will always be victims of deception. Our existence has been stunted so far because of our blind beliefs with passive capitulation.*

Like Raawat the elephant, we are caught in a web of beliefs built around our minds and bodies by society.

Upgraditis

·········● ● ● ● ● ● ● ● ● ● ●·········

Once a Catholic, Hindu and Buddhist priests were exhausted from endless debates about their beliefs. They wanted to settle the debate once for all. So they decided to test; they agreed on a method to determine the power of their beliefs. They must each jump off a cliff and chant the name of their respective saviour. Whoever lands safe wins; they worked out the jumping order and agreed that they all have to jump high up first to clear the cliff cleanly.

The Buddhist priest was first to jump.

On the way up, He chanted Buddha, Buddha, Buddha, Buddha, Buddha...

On the way down: He chanted Buddha, Buddha ...

He landed on the rocks 200 feet below and instantly turned into tomato salsa. Watching this shocking incident, the remaining two agreed the test must go on.

It was now the Hindu priests turn. He jumped and closed his eyes.

On the way up: He chanted Krishna, Krishna, Krishna, Krishna, Krishna.

On the way down: He chanted Krishna, Krishna...

Upgraditis

Something unique happened. The Hindu priest started levitating and stopped midair; he opened his eyes, floated back on top of the cliff, and landed safely beside the Catholic priest, followed by an awkward moment of silence.

Now it was the Catholic priest's turn to jump off the cliff; he gathered all the courage and started running and then jumping high up in the air.

On the way up, He chanted Jesus, Jesus, Jesus, Jesus, Jesus.

On the way down, Jesus, Jesus.

He noticed in horror that he was not slowing down, so he started chanting Krishna, Krishna, Krishna, Krishna, Krishna.

·············••••••••··········

> *A person will be enslaved in some form*
> *as long as they believe that someone else*
> *can take them to the objective truth. These*
> *individuals will escape from one belief and*
> *get trapped in another; they will never be free.*
> *Belief switching only provides short term*
> *relief, but it's just a shift in the weight from*
> *one shoulder to another.*

Upgraditis

Do not believe, instead seek. Become a seeker.

Belief is a barrier, and seeking is the bridge. If people believe in something blindly, they will not understand it correctly. So instead, learn how to seek, learn, and accept that everyone could be wrong. Belief is a dead body. You can carry it around as long as you like - it is an unnecessary burden that doesn't bring any joy. After some time, this dead body will start to rot and start stinking. It is not healthy to keep the company of the deceased. With your beliefs, you are just carrying dead old knowledge from others. Look at some of the superstitions that are still prevalent in our society. The original source of all this bullshit is unknown and will never be known.

We need to take all the beliefs from our lives and replace them with doubts because doubt leads to inquiry; it takes you to a new adventure, it doesn't mind questions. Doubt will never allow you to be ignorant for a long time; it will find the light. You need to be honest with yourself; do you know it or not? Can you do it or not? So don't let any beliefs rest in your mind.

Upgraditis

Belief poisons everything; it suffocates the truth and resuscitates ignorance and delusion. Therefore, any statement made with a belief is untrue or anti-truth. Belief is the building block of every religion; doubt is the building block of science. That is why both can't be bridged.

Belief is completely unnatural as humans are not born with any beliefs but curiosity and doubt. So doubt is natural to humans. Doubt doesn't mean disbelief; disbelief is inverted belief; just like the Atheist and Theist are the same; travelling in the same bus called «ist» or «ism».

Another lie that society feeds in your head is to "believe in yourself", which is utter nonsense. Belief requires at least two entities; If you want these two entities within yourself, then this will result in some form of mental illness. If you really become two entities, people will call you schizophrenic. How many people live within your body? If you go around and start saying

Upgraditis

I respect and admire myself. People would think you are a narcissist. As respecting or admiring requires at least two entities. The same is true for believing. I believe in myself is a false narrative; instead, replace this with confidence. If you are confident about your skills and talent, the world will notice and respect you.

The elephant in the introduction was destroyed by a belief system. The training crush had an impact on the curiosity and sense of knowing. In a similar vein, this is occurring with humans. It happened to me, and I have no doubt that it is also happening to you. Society conditioned us to believe in self-limiting beliefs to be enslaved and remain poor and powerless. Your life's goal should be to ensure that all of your beliefs are extinguished quietly. Once all of your beliefs are peacefully extinguished, you will feel liberated, calmer, more curious about the world, and you will gain a greater understanding.

Doubt is suppressed by belief systems. Your belief systems will lead you to a state of intellectual impotence. I'm not sure what happened to Raawat, the elephant, to be honest with you. That elephant was never seen by me again. Did that elephant ever manage to free itself from the shackles of its beliefs? This remains a mystery.

Upgraditis

As our journey in this book is about to end, I would like to remind everyone that:

- Do not believe in luck; seek talent and skills.
- Do not believe in happiness; seek peace.
- Do not believe in equity; seek equality.
- Do not believe in industrial education; seek creativity.
- Do not believe in Hollywood love; seek a blissful state.
- Do not believe in perfection; seek completeness.
- Do not believe that technology connects; seek real connections.
- Do not believe in the cage; seek freedom.
- Doubt mental illness; seek your mental-ableness.
- Do not believe; instead, verify, doubt and seek.

Upgraditis

Intelligence is essential for our existence on this planet. However, the true nature of intelligence doesn't believe; it is curious; it doubts; it validates; it verifies and doesn't trust. Your intelligence has a thirst for knowledge; you create an environment for your intelligence to operate with complete freedom, then you will know that it hates believing in anyone or anything. So, I ask you to switch off belief mode and turn on intelligence mode. Runaway from the people who believe they have found the truth; follow the one seeking it.

ABOUT THE AUTHOR

Sandeep Babbar is a very attractive man who currently resides in Australia; he moved here from the land of Yoga, Butter Chicken and Kamasutra in the early 2000s.

Sandeep's purpose in life is to be useful. He likes to speak and write about applying modern wisdom in business and personal life. In addition, he loves to coach individuals suffering from mental health issues.

He is an engineer, a technologist, a storyteller and he has recently been named as the most interesting man on the planet.

www.ingramcontent.com/pod-product-compliance
Lightning Source LLC
Chambersburg PA
CBHW070252010526
44107CB00056B/2439